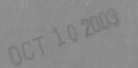

Photographic Credits

Farshid Assassi: cover, pages 115-116, 118-121, 129, 145-147, 152-153, 160-162, 164 (left), 165-167, 172-173, 175 (right), 176, 194, 197, 200, 207, 210-215, 219, 223, 228
Daniel Bibb: pages 4-13, 109-113, 126-127, 130-131, 134 (bottom row right), 136, 138-143, 148-151, 154-158, 168-169, 171, 179 (right), 181, 188-193, 195, 201-203, 206, 208-209, 224, 226-227, 244-254, backcover
Timothy Hursley: pages 21, 28, 124-125, 128, 132-133, 137, 159, 170, 174, 175 (left), 177-178, 179 (left), 180, 182-183, 185, 204, 220-221, 231

Abbott-Boyle, Inc. Photographers: pages102-105
Colin Goldie: pages 30 (bottom middle), 58 (top right and bottom)
Tim Griffith: page 29 (top row and right)
Kan Studios: page 30 (bottom right)
Steve Keating: pages 42, 45 (top right and bottom), 46, 51 (left and top right and bottom), 55 (top right), 56, 59, 60 (bottom), 63-64, 65 (center top and bottom)
John Lodge: pages 29 (bottom middle), 30 (bottom left)
Steven McConnell: pages 34-35, 45 (top left), 51 (top middle), 58 (top left), 60 (top), 65 (right), 88-101, 108, 114, 117, 122-123, 134 (bottom row left), 135, 163, 164 (right), 184, 186-187, 196, 198-199, 218, 222, 225, 229, 232, 234-237
NBBJ Archives: pages 32-33, 240-241
Lisa Pascarelli: Oscar Riera Ojeda's back cover flap portrait
Reebok Archives: pages 24-27, 230
Maria Ryan Wagner: pages 30 (top right), 31
Paul Warchol: page 29 (bottom left)
Scott Wyatt: pages 134 (top row), 233

Publications

Architecture
June 1998
"On the Boards: NBBJ-Reebok World Headquarters"

Space
June 1998
"World Headquarters for Reebok International, Ltd."

Architectural Record
July 1999
"Desks, Phones, Basketball Court: Reebok's New World Headquarters"

Bauwelt
September 1999
"Reebok Headquarters"

Parking Today
October 1999
"Reebok Opts for Play Fields Instead of Pavement"

Business Facilities
October 1999
"Field of Dreams"

Corporate Real Estate Strategies
November 1999
"Reebok Running with New Campus"

Casabella
January 2000
"Reebok's New World Headquarters"

The Patriot Ledger
March 24, 2000
"Reebok's Canton building on target"

High Profile
April 2000
"Reebok International World Headquarters Nears Completion"

Footwear News
June 5, 2000
"Reebok new headquarters combines business, pleasure"

Architecture
September 2000
Fast Companies: Computer power gave NBBJ the stamina to deliver the new "Reebok headquarters in record time"

The Patriot Ledger
September 8, 2000
"Building adopts sleek design"

Boston Globe
September 8, 2000
"Rebuilding Reebok"

Boston Herald
September 8, 2000
"Reebok, its wandering over, discovers itself"

Structures
October 2000
"Fast Track to Company Culture"

Neponset Valley Daily News
October 19, 2000
"Reebok Ready for Future: Sports apparel company's new Canton headquarters reflects its outlook"

Boston Herald
December 3, 2000
"Reebok HQ fun, functional and removed from city rhythms"

Metropolis
January 2001
"Reebok Redux"

Architektur Für Sport
January 2001
"Reebok World Headquarters"

Building Design and Construction
January 2001
"Sports Spectacular: New Reebok International headquarters projects an active image"

Interior Construction
February 15, 2001
"Hunter Douglas and Central Ceilings help keep Reebok running"

Tasarim
August 2001
"Reebok World Headquarters"

Massage Magazine
August 15, 2001
"Reebok promotes wellness"

Boston Herald
November 2, 2001
"Mover and Shakers: AGC Award"

Boston Herald
December 28, 2001
"BOMA Building of the Year Award Winners"

New England Construction Review
January 2002
"Reebok World Headquarters"

Columbus Business Journal
January 25, 2002
"NBBJ design for Reebok honored"

Architectural Record
February 2002
"Getting onto the digital fast track"

Architectural Record
February 2002
"Fast track construction becomes the norm"

Puget Sound Business Journal
March 21, 2002
"Reebok receives accolades"

Athletic Business
June 2002
"Sports And Fitness Center at Reebok"

Competitions
Summer 2002
"NBBJ - Reebok World Headquarters"

Acknowledgements

This project was realized as a result of the inspiration, vision and commitment of numerous remarkable people. In particular, we would like to acknowledge the following individuals for their unique and valued roles in launching a new era for Reebok.

Representing Reebok International: Paul Fireman, Chairman, President and CEO; Douglas Noonan, P.E., Director of Corporate Real Estate & Facilities; and Edward Rybak, AIA, Facility, Planning & Design Manager. Representing The Commonwealth of Massachusetts: The Honorable Argeo Paul Celucci, Former Governor. Representing the City of Boston: The Honorable Thomas Menino, Mayor. Representing the Township of Canton: The Honorable Avril Elkort, Chairperson, Board of Selectmen; and Thomas Clarke, Chairperson, Canton Association of Industries. Finally, representing the numerous trades people, suppliers and contractors and their unwavering commitment to construction excellence: Charles Buuck, Senior Vice President and New England Regional Manager, Turner Construction; Bruce Ventura, Chief Estimator, Turner Construction; and Thomas O'Connor, Jr., President, O'Connor Constructors.

Thanks and appreciation as well to the author of the chapter text for this book: Bonnie Duncan, with Morgan Coleman.

Photographers

Farshid Assassi

Based in Santa Barbara, California, Farshid has worked throughout the United States, Europe and Australia, to provide photography that brings recognition to the premier architecture of our time. His insistence on perfection and his critical eye for composition, color and balance have played a critical role in the development of architectural photography. For the past twenty-five years, his work has appeared in national and international design publications, elevating our understanding and appreciation of both photography and architecture.

Tim Hursley

An internationally renowned architectural photographer, Tim lives in Little Rock, Arkansas, and regularly contributes to the national and international design press. His work is rooted in the significance of space to the human experience. Recently, he co-authored a book with Andrea Oppenheimer-Dean titled, Rural Studio: Samuel Mockbee and An Architecture of Decency.

Daniel Bibb

Based in New York City, Daniel is an architecture and design photographer. Among his most recent published books are a monograph on the work of Boston architects Nader Tehrani and Mónica Ponce de León from Office dA, and a poetic compilation of New York women and the contents of their bags, for fashion designer Kate Spade. He is also a continuing contributor to numerous architecture and interior design magazines. Dan Bibb is a graduate of the Museum School in Boston and continues to pursue still life work for publishing and advertising.

Project Facts

* located in Canton, Massachusetts, nearly 15 miles south of Boston
* 44 acres of total land area
* 36 acres of green space
* 522,000 sq ft gross building area
* 1-acre storm water detention pond for irrigation and developing a wetlands
* four 100,000 sq ft office buildings
* 13,000 sq ft meeting and exhibit hall
* 30,000 sq ft fitness center
* 8,500 sq ft cafeteria, featuring a sidewalk cafe and formal dining area
* 18,000 sq ft renovated historic guest house
* 10,000 sq ft childcare center (unbuilt)
* two 4-story parking garages totaling 351,000 sq ft and 1,431 parking spaces
* 33 handicapped parking spaces within the Reebok site
* 520-ft-long, 60-ft-high glass circulation spine
* 51,000 sq ft of articulated glass window wall
* 20,000 lites of glass in the window wall
* 110 different types of light fixtures
* 5,000 sq ft of composite aluminum
* over 5,000 dimension control points
* 18 stairways
* more than a mile of handrails
* 13 elevators
* 43 entry/exit points
* 38 rest rooms
* 20 drinking fountains
* regulation Little League baseball field
* recreational softball field

* regulation soccer pitch
* regulation NBA basketball court
* sand volleyball court
* two tennis courts featuring new plexi surface
* 400-meter Olympic running track
* rural jogging trails
* four acres of lawn space for sports expositions and demonstrations

Awards

Honor Award for Design Excellence
AIA, Boston Society of Architects, 2001

Office Building of the Year
BOMA-New England Chapter, 2001

Award Winner
Build Massachusetts, 2001

Award Winner
Associated General Contractors of Massachusetts, 2001

American Architecture Award
Chicago Athenaeum, 2000

Award of Commendation
AIA, Seattle Chapter, 2000

Nick Charles
Senior Technical Architect

Nick's notable skill as a technical architect contributes to the success of highly complex projects such as corporate headquarters, theaters and hospitals. As the technical lead for his studio, Nick sets the quality control standards for each project, and is responsible for developing the technical expertise of his colleagues. The most important aspect of his role is to understand the needs of the client, and insure that systems and design functionally achieve the vision.

Jin Ah Park
Project Designer

Jin Ah is a dynamic design leader who has inspired numerous teams to achieve high levels of creativity and profession-alism. Her earlier background, involving small-scale projects, brings a unique perspective to her macro-scale work at NBBJ. She has been a key member of successful project teams around the world, including the Manggarai Integrated Transportation Terminal in Jakarta, Indonesia, TelenorHeadquarters in Oslo, Norway (the largest telecommu-nications company in Scandinavia), and an office tower in Barcelona, Spain. Her advanced skills in digital media allow her designs to achieve a holistic approach from the presentation graphics to the 3-D computer models of construction details. Jin Ah recently relocated from the Oslo office to the London office, helping to develop NBBJ's practice in Europe.

Ruben Gonzalez
Construction Administration Lead

As technical architect and construction administrator, Ruben works through the design and documentation phases of projects, then follows through during construction on-site. His leadership in the development of contract documents benefits from hands-on experience with construction standards, methods, and techniques. Ruben's role as the on-site problem-solver assures smooth construction coordination and expedites the cost-effective execution of the project. His thorough understanding of agency coordination, both during documentation and construction, facilitates strong working relationships with public agency officials.

Chris Larson
Senior Project Designer—Interiors

Chris's thorough problem-solving analysis of each interior project produces fresh solutions and innovative approaches for his clients. He is accustomed to working on projects from beginning to end—from initiation of the idea through installation. An industry leader in the creative use of light, color, and texture, Chris distinguishes space with variety, interest, and excitement. His success in providing functionally efficient, as well as aesthetically satisfying designs is reflected in the rich diversity of his projects.

Alan Young
Senior Project Architect—Interiors

Alan's designs have earned wide recognition, including Burger King International Headquarters in Miami, and Turner Construction's new headquarters in Seattle. His colleagues and clients respect him as a passionate visionary, collaborator, and leader. He is known as a well-rounded, innovative thinker with a keen sense for integrating technology, process and design. Currently, Alan is leading one of NBBJ's largest integrated interior architecture projects, Immunex Corporate Headquarters in Seattle.

Dave Burger
Senior Technical Architect—Interiors

Dave's strongest asset is his flexibility, given his broad range of project types, from single family and multi-family residential projects to high-rises, and from new construction to renovations. His leadership, technical expertise and attention to details are characteristics ideally suited to his role as a senior technical architect. One of his greatest strengths is his ability to maintain the integrity of the design concept during the detailing and construction of the building. Recent projects include The Reebok World Headquarters, and The Teledesic Corporate Headquarters.

Rick Buckley, AIA
Partner-in-Charge of Design—Competition

Rick is one of NBBJ's most talented designers, highly regarded by clients for his ability to engage them in the design process. His innovative vision and exceptional leadership are instrumental to the firm's success, both past and present. His broad range of experience encompasses residential, mixed use, commercial office buildings, historic renovation, performing arts theaters, luxury hotels, and resorts. Rick's numerous projects include the Paramount Theatre renovation in Seattle, the Seattle Downtown Retail Core Redevelopment, Sun Mountain Resort in Winthrop, Washington, Fluke Hall on the University of Washington campus, Fuxing Mansion in Shanghai, and Kangbuk Samsung Hospital in Seoul.

NBBJ's multidisciplinary design practice includes expertise in architecture, planning, urban design, interiors, lighting, graphics, and interactive design. The firm continues to expand, diversify, define and explore as an international design practice. With nearly 800 professionals in five national and four international offices, NBBJ ranks as the country's second largest and the world's fifth largest architectural firm.

What sets NBBJ apart is the ability to combine the best attributes of both a large and small firm. In terms of size, the firm's resource base is enormous. At the same time, its system of specialized studios within the larger structure ensures that clients receive personalized service. Each studio, made up of 30 to 60 individuals, combines complementary skills in formal design, functional design, building systems design, and process design. From pre-design to occupancy, projects continue under the control of a single core team responsible to the client.

NBBJ's multidisciplinary talent complements the firm's strong origins in architecture. The integration of diverse capabilities produces a comprehensive blend that fosters our clients' visions. With a distinguished inventory of accomplishments, NBBJ has received more than 300 national and international design awards.

Highlighting the firm's rich portfolio, strong practices have been established in corporate and commercial, health-care, and sports and entertainment design. The studios also provide design expertise for airports, retail, government buildings, campus planning, research and advanced technology facilities, urban planning, and senior living.

NBBJ holds that a dynamic client deserves a dynamic, high-energy design team. This means providing a strong service orientation, flexible attitude, and the technical knowledge to pursue innovation with confidence. It is a team that knows the limits of what is possible, but also has the resources, strength and drive to achieve something original.

Founded in 1943 by four Seattle architects, Naramore, Bain, Brady, and Johanson, NBBJ now has U.S. offices in Seattle, San Francisco, Los Angeles, Columbus, New York, and international offices in London, Oslo, Beijing, and Taipei.

Scott Wyatt, FAIA
Partner-in-Charge

Scott's work, primarily with corporate clients, is distinguished by a unique ability to translate the firm's vision, purpose, and culture into design, creating elegant facilities that integrate interiors with building structure, character, and landscape. He has led projects for some of the nation's foremost corporations, establishing environments whose accessibility, comfort, and meaning serve to enhance creativity and productivity. His touchstones for designing a space are to acknowledge and promote the client's identity, character of leadership, services and products, reputation, and position within the given market.

Steven McConnell, AIA
Design Principal-in-Charge

Steve's work is inspired by the belief that contemporary architecture provides physical form to the aspirations of his client's enterprise. Since joining NBBJ in 1990, he has led the design and planning of select projects including The Residences at Liberty, New Jersey, Samsung's Global Gateway in Korea, Swedish Medical Center South Tower in Seattle, and the new United States Federal Courthouse also in Seattle. Prior to joining NBBJ, he worked in Tokyo for Arata Isozaki, leading the Kashi Twin Towers project in Fukuoka, Japan. Steve develops and applies innovative team strategies that enable extraordinary performance. Collaborative interaction, intentional action, inclusive reasoning, focusing on a dynamic reality, and cultivation of the best ideas are the values that underpin his leadership model: Process Design. Steve is a board member of the Seattle Children's Museum and of Homes Without Boundaries, which involves over 200 Seattle youth each year building essential housing in Mexico.

K. Robert Swartz
Principal

Rob brings extensive corporate real estate expertise to NBBJ. This perspective strengthens the firm's approach to client service and brings an understanding of the complete real estate lifecycle to projects. Rob's experience allows him to craft design solutions that are closely integrated with NBBJ's clients and their long-term business goals. His experience in strategic planning and portfolio management rounds out NBBJ's services, informs the design process, and increases the firm's ability to produce value-added results.

Jonathan Ward
Senior Project Designer

Jonathan joined NBBJ in 1996 and brings a significant range of expertise in urban and international projects. This experience involves work in North and South America, North and Southeast Asia, Russia, and Europe. Jonathan has led design teams noted for innovative concepts, from the first competition sketch to the completed project. He has been instrumental in developing the use of computer technology for design, creating new opportunities and improv-ing delivery capabilities. His facility for using technology as a means to commu-nicate designs, whether to clients, the building team or the public, has greatly expedited large and complex building projects. Jonathan recently relocated from NBBJ's Oslo office to help estab-lish the firm's new London practice.

Project Data

Name

Reebok World Headquarters

Owner

Reebok International, Ltd.

Location

Canton, Massachusetts

Credits

Architect

NBBJ
111 South Jackson Street
Seattle, WA 98104
206-223-5555

Design Team

Scott Wyatt (Partner-in-charge); Steven McConnell (Design Principal-in charge); K. Robert Swartz (Principal); Jonathan Ward (Senior Project Designer); Nick Charles (Senior Technical Architect); Ruben Gonzalez (Construction Administration Lead); Jin Ah Park, Andy Bromberg (Project Designers); Gary Schaefer (Senior Project Architect); Chris Larson (Senior Project Designer-interiors); Alan Young (Senior Project Architect-interiors); Dave Burger (Senior Technical Architect-interiors); Richard G. Buckley (Partner-in-charge of Design-competition); Joey Myers (Project Designer-competition); Diane Anderson, Rob Anderson, Daniel Beyer, Frances Cirillo, Daniel Cockrell, Case Creal, Tessie Dantes-Era, Susan Dewey, Yumiko Fujimori, Roddy Grant, Jay Halleran, Cecile Haw, Lisa Harrington, Cory Harris, Shiki Huangyutitham, Michael Kreiss, Dave Kutsunai, John Millard, Terrance O'Neil, Sarah Pelone, Ligang Qiu, Leo Raymundo, Joe Rettenmaier, Derek Ryan, Janet Samples, Amy Sparks, Rae Ann Stewart, Carsten Stinn, Trisna Tanus, Alec Vassiliadis (Project Team).

Office Systems and Furniture Design

Archideas

Landscape Architect

EDAW

Lighting Design

Jeffrey I. L. Miller, IALD

Engineers

Vanasse Hangen Brustlin, Inc. (civil, traffic, permitting); McNamara/Salvia, Inc. (structural); Cosentini Associates (mechanical, electrical, plumbing, fireproofing); McPhail Associates, Inc. (geotechnical).

Consultants

Advanced Structures Incorporated (curtain wall design and structure); RWDI (fluid dynamic modeling); Cavanaugh & Tocci (acoustic design); Schirmer (code analysis); Lerch Bates (elevator design); Crabtree & McGrath (food service design); William Hook (architectural illustration); Gilbert Gorski (architectural illustration); B+B Models (precision models).

General Contractors

Turner/O'Connor – a joint venture

Turner Construction
2 Seaport Land
Second Floor
Boston, Massachusetts
617-247-6400

O'Connor Constructors
45 Industrial Drive
Canton, MA
617-364-9000

Specifics

Building Area

522,000 square feet

Date of Competition

September 1997

Date of Design

October 1997- June 1998

Date of Completion

June 2000

designers

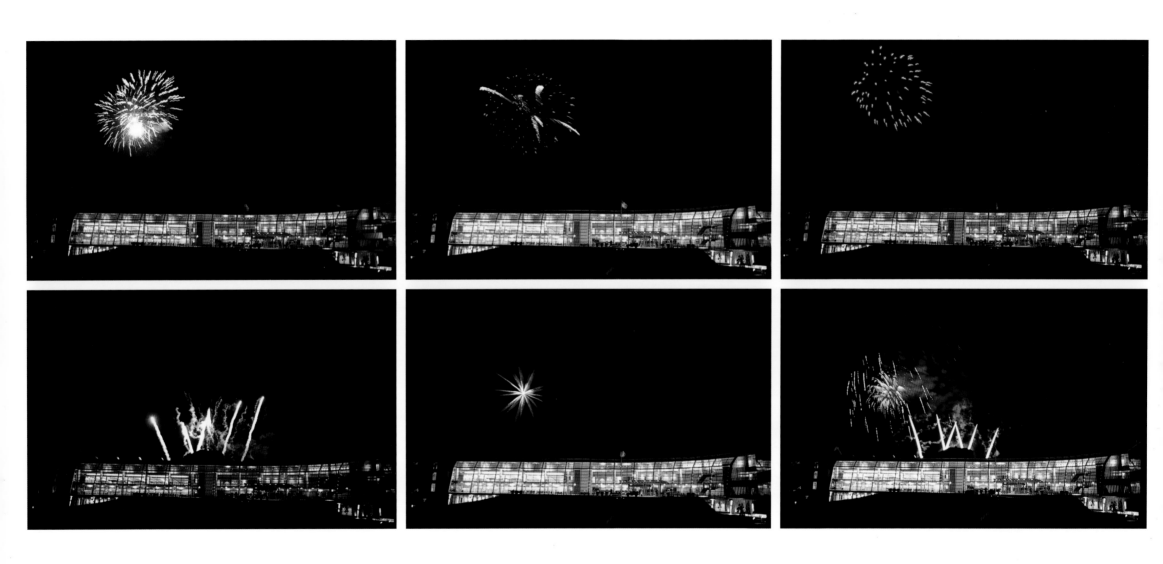

below / opposite page Grand opening celebration and
activities, September 20, 2000.
/ Corporate social event.

Reebok World Headquarters' visitors at
entry plaza; innovative products display;
and promotional marketing activities with
headquarters as a backdrop. / Grand
opening celebration and activities,
September 20, 2000.

below / opposite page   Youth soccer activities inspire
Reebok professionals from within
their offices beyond.

below / opposite page Play fields at Reebok are available
for community activities such as little
league baseball.

NBBJ's design of the new corporate headquarters for Reebok is the physical manifestation of the company's inspiring values: explosive creativity and innovation. The design is defined by a clear understanding of the collective power of all the activities and sports that form the stage for the changing and expanding array of Reebok products. ■ In architectural terms, this translates to spaces that convey the energy of the company and relate to a landscape inspired by a tapestry of sporting surfaces. Expansive views call attention to athletic possibilities and natural greenery as elements in the design composition. In turn, the environment becomes the creative domain that inspires the evolution of Reebok's products and sets a high standard that profoundly influences the attitude and motivation of all who encounter it. ■ The connection binding the campus to its site reflects the unity and balance between the individual and the team, and between sports and nature. In much the same spirit as the long distance runner, the new headquarters meets the ground, presses into it, and flies over it. Like a runner poised on the blocks, there is a sense of the physical tension felt just before uncoiling and running the race. Gravity and nature root the athlete's body as the shoe carves into the dirt leaving a furrow of soil—the imprint of a person interacting with nature. The architecture similarly expresses a sense of motion balanced with solid rooted elements and light flowing forms that sail over the site. ■ The project's principle elements are linked by an undulating glass circulation spine that doubles as an expansive atrium and, in form, suggests the bowl of an Olympic stadium. It offers a multi-level experience of connectivity. As the literal and figurative backbone of the campus, the spine provides stability and focus to the movement and energy of the headquarters complex. At one point, it expands to provide the main lobby arrival hall, a soaring exhilarating space. In addition, the spine features an NBA-scale basketball court. ■ From any vantage point within the spine, people see balconies, showrooms, runners passing by, outdoor sports activities and employees at work. The spine allows a vital flow of activity that makes clear, "this is Reebok." Supported by a structural core of pre-cast elements anchored in the ground, the curving structure appears to float above the site, branching into four sections housing company divisions. This branching plan embraces and articulates the large fields and activity areas around the complex. ■ Designed to incorporate flexibility in contemporary office planning, the four office wings are spaced by support functions (including auditoriums, conference centers, and showrooms) that are fundamental to the development, presentation, and sale of Reebok products. Working in close physical proximity to the product was deemed essential to Reebok's business environment, and team formation is unconstrained by the architecture. ■ The transparency of the spine's faceted curtain wall visually and metaphorically breaks down barriers, blurring the boundaries between interior and exterior. A terrace provides views of the outdoor playing fields, the indoor basketball court, and the running tracks below, integrating athletic activities with the workplace and constantly reinforcing the company's identity. In the spine Reebok organizes parties, employees enjoy the fitness center, and designers interact to develop their ideas, whether intentionally or by chance. ■ Together, these elements link and motivate all aspects of Reebok and its culture. The unexpected squeak of a basketball shoe in the distance provides sudden clarity, reflecting a place where employees and the essence of their work converge and energize each other.

chapter six

transformation

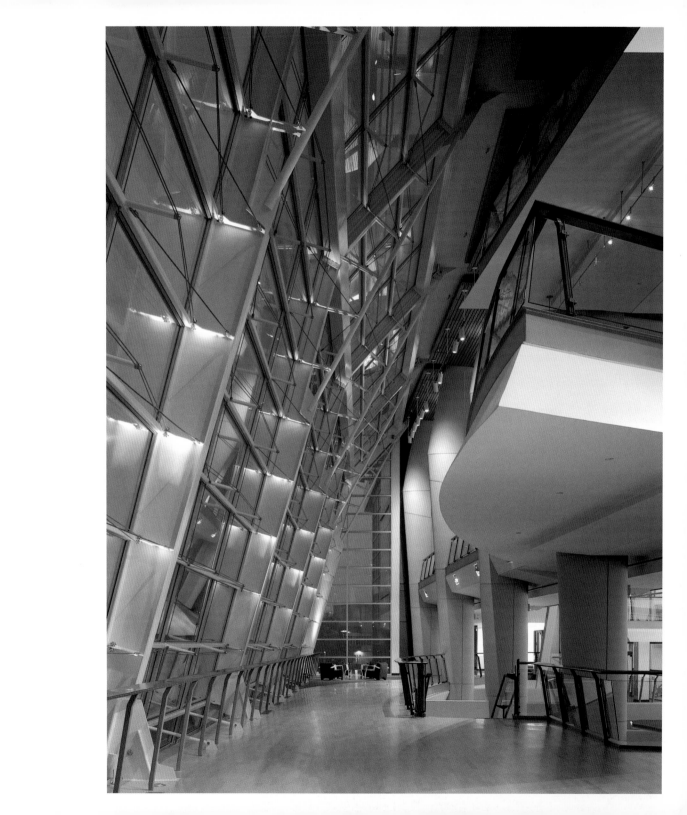

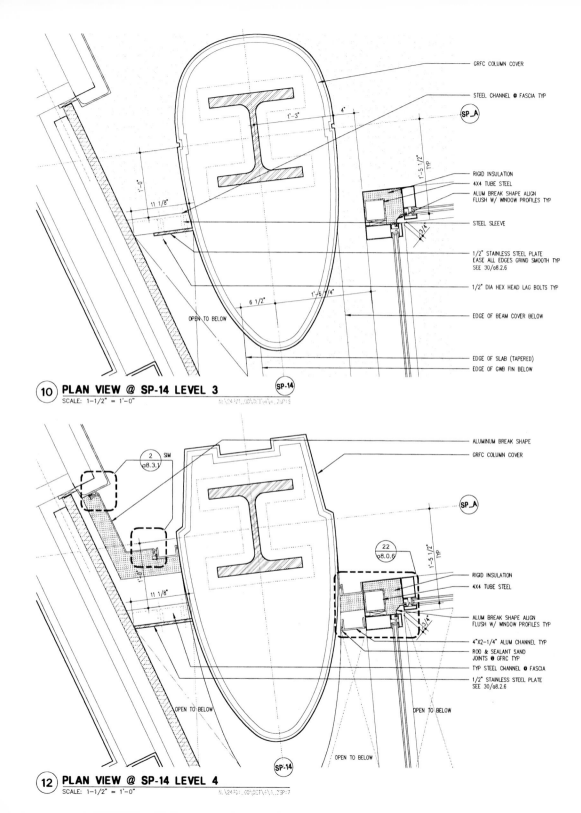

GRFC COLUMN COVER

STEEL CHANNEL @ FASCIA TYP

SP_A

1'-3"   4"

1'-5 1/2" TYP

RIGID INSULATION
4X4 TUBE STEEL
ALUM BREAK SHAPE ALIGN
FLUSH W/ WINDOW PROFILES TYP

STEEL SLEEVE

11 1/8"

1'-0"

3/4"

1/2" STAINLESS STEEL PLATE
EASE ALL EDGES GRIND SMOOTH TYP
SEE 30/ø8.2.6

1/2" DIA HEX HEAD LAG BOLTS TYP

EDGE OF BEAM COVER BELOW

OPEN TO BELOW

6 1/2"   1'-6 1/4"

EDGE OF SLAB (TAPERED)
EDGE OF GWB FIN BELOW

10 **PLAN VIEW @ SP-14 LEVEL 3**
SCALE: 1-1/2" = 1'-0"   SP-14

ALUMINUM BREAK SHAPE
GRFC COLUMN COVER

2 SIM
ø8.3.1

SP_A

1'-5 1/2" TYP

22
ø8.0.6

RIGID INSULATION
4X4 TUBE STEEL

11 1/8"

3/4"

ALUM BREAK SHAPE ALIGN
FLUSH W/ WINDOW PROFILES TYP

4"X2-1/4" ALUM CHANNEL TYP
ROD & SEALANT SAND
JOINTS @ GFRC TYP
TYP STEEL CHANNEL @ FASCIA
1/2" STAINLESS STEEL PLATE
SEE 30/ø8.2.6

OPEN TO BELOW

OPEN TO BELOW

OPEN TO BELOW

12 **PLAN VIEW @ SP-14 LEVEL 4**
SCALE: 1-1/2" = 1'-0"

below / opposite page /   Column enclosure construction documents
following spread   and detail view. / Spine interior view
                          from level three. / Stair detail, and
                          spine interior view.

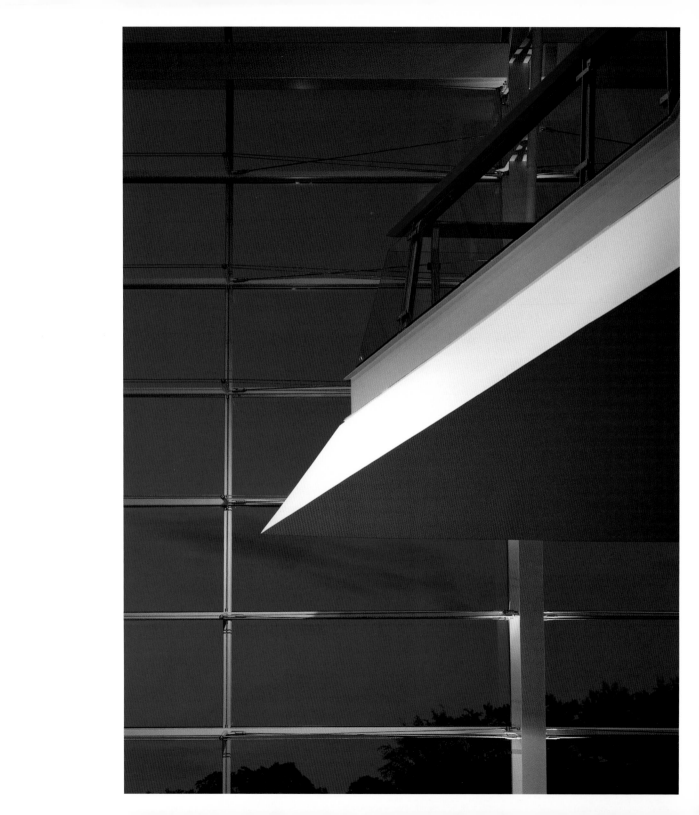

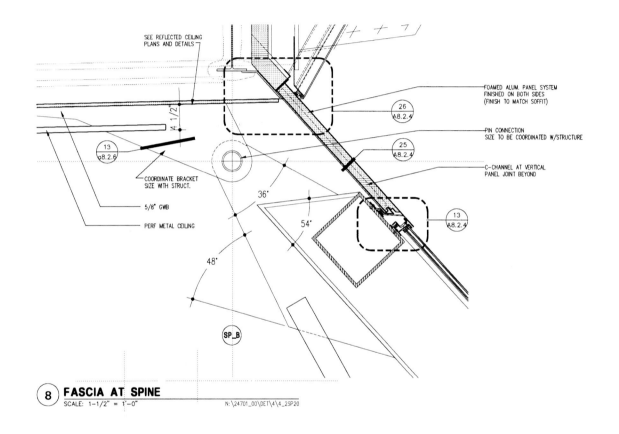

SEE REFLECTED CEILING
PLANS AND DETAILS

FOAMED ALUM. PANEL SYSTEM
FINISHED ON BOTH SIDES
(FINISH TO MATCH SOFFIT)

26
A8.2.4

PIN CONNECTION
SIZE TO BE COORDINATED W/STRUCTURE

25
A8.2.4

C-CHANNEL AT VERTICAL
PANEL JOINT BEYOND

13
A8.2.6

COORDINATE BRACKET
SIZE WITH STRUCT.

5/8" GWB

PERF METAL CEILING

4 1/2"

36°

54°

48°

13
A8.2.4

SP_B

8 **FASCIA AT SPINE**
SCALE: 1-1/2" = 1'-0"   N:\24701_00\DET\4\4_2SP20

below / opposite page Bridge handrail, fascia and roof
construction documents. / Spine
enclosure termination.

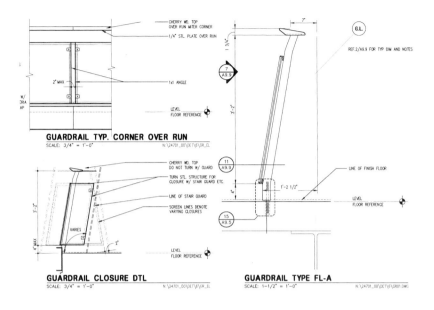

CHERRY WD. TOP
OVER RUN MITER CORNER
1/4" STL. PLATE OVER RUN

2" MAX
1x1 ANGLE

LEVEL
FLOOR REFERENCE

GUARDRAIL TYP. CORNER OVER RUN
SCALE: 3/4" = 1'-0"   N:\24701_00\DET\6\GR_EL

CHERRY WD. TOP
DO NOT TURN W/ GUARD
TURN STL STRUCTURE FOR
CLOSURE W/ STAIR GUARD ETC.
LINE OF STAIR GUARD
SCREEN LINES DENOTE
VARYING CLOSURES

VARIES

LEVEL
FLOOR REFERENCE

GUARDRAIL CLOSURE DTL
SCALE: 3/4" = 1'-0"   N:\24701_00\DET\6\GR_EL

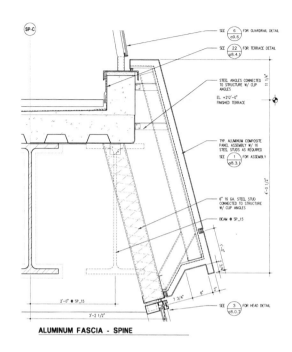

G.L.

REF.2/A9.9 FOR TYP DIM AND NOTES

7
A9.9

LINE OF FINISH FLOOR

1'-2 1/2"

LEVEL
FLOOR REFERENCE

11
A9.9

15
A9.5

GUARDRAIL TYPE FL-A
SCALE: 1-1/2" = 1'-0"   N:\24701_00\DET\6\GR01.DWG

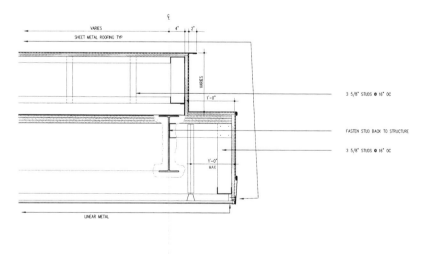

SP-C

SEE 6 FOR GUARDRAIL DETAIL
a9.5

SEE 22 FOR TERRACE DETAIL
a8.4

STEEL ANGLES CONNECTED
TO STRUCTURE W/ CLIP
ANGLES

EL +2'12'-0"
FINISHED TERRACE

TYP. ALUMINUM COMPOSITE
PANEL ASSEMBLY W/ 16
STEEL STUDS AS REQUIRED
SEE 1 FOR ASSEMBLY
a8.3.1

6" 16 GA. STEEL STUD
CONNECTED TO STRUCTURE
W/ CLIP ANGLES

BEAM @ SP_15

2'-0" @ SP_15
3'-2 1/2"

SEE 3 FOR HEAD DETAIL
a8.0

ALUMINUM FASCIA - SPINE

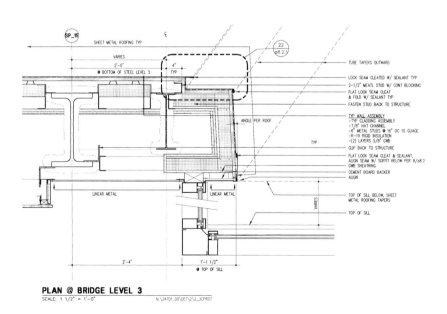

SP_15

SHEET METAL ROOFING TYP

22
a8.2.1

VARIES
2'-0"
@ BOTTOM OF STEEL LEVEL 3
4"   TYP

TUBE TAPERS OUTWARD

LOCK SEAM CLEATED W/ SEALANT TYP
2-1/2" MEATL STUD W/ CONT BLOCKING
FLAT LOCK SEAM CLEAT
& FOLD W/ SEALANT TYP
FASTEN STUD BACK TO STRUCTURE
TYP WALL ASSEMBLY
-TYP CLADDING ASSEMBLY
-7/8" HAT CHANNEL
-6" METAL STUDS @ 16" OC 16 GUAGE
-R-19 RIGID INSULATION
-(2) LAYERS 5/8" GWB
CLIP BACK TO STRUCTURE
FLAT LOCK SEAM CLEAT & SEALANT,
ALIGN SEAM W/ SOFFIT BELOW PER 8/a8.3
GWB SHEATHING
CEMENT BOARD BACKER
ALIGN
TOP OF SILL BELOW, SHEET
METAL ROOFING TAPERS
TOP OF SILL

ANGLE PER ROOF

TYP

LINEAR METAL   LINEAR METAL

VARIES

2'-4"   1'-1 1/2"
@ TOP OF SILL

PLAN @ BRIDGE LEVEL 3
SCALE: 1 1/2" = 1'-0"   N:\24701_00\DET\2\2_3CPR07

VARIES   4"   2"
SHEET METAL ROOFING TYP

VARIES

3 5/8" STUDS @ 16" OC

1'-0"

FASTEN STUD BACK TO STRUCTURE

3 5/8" STUDS @ 16" OC

1'-0"
MAX

LINEAR METAL

SECTION @ BRIDGE BUILT UP CURB

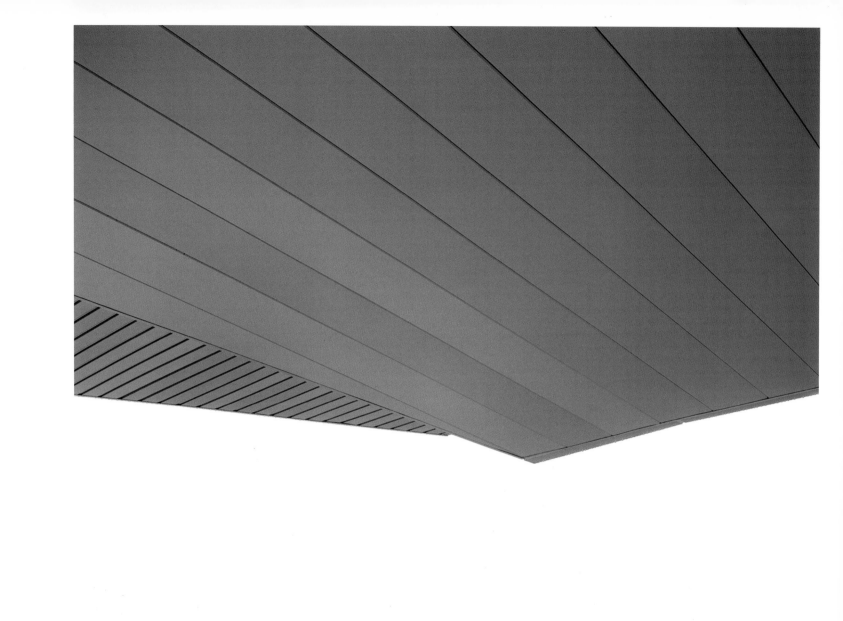

An honest image. It is the

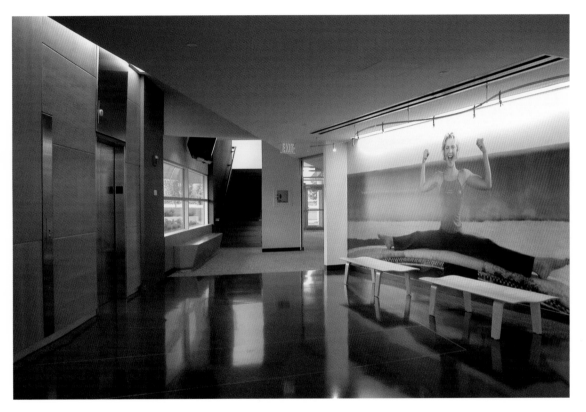

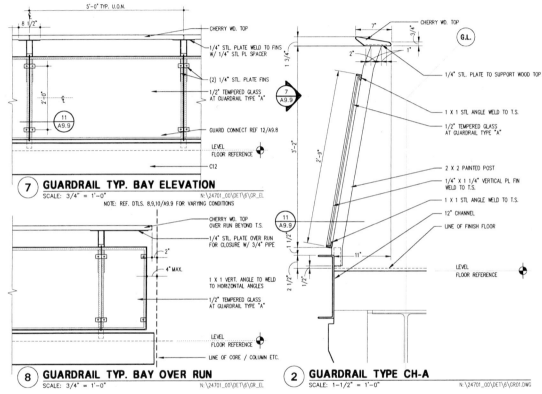

7 GUARDRAIL TYP. BAY ELEVATION
SCALE: 3/4" = 1'-0"   N:\24701_00\DET\6\GR_EL
NOTE: REF. DTLS. 8,9,10/A9.9 FOR VARYING CONDITIONS

8 GUARDRAIL TYP. BAY OVER RUN
SCALE: 3/4" = 1'-0"   N:\24701_00\DET\6\GR_EL

2 GUARDRAIL TYPE CH-A
SCALE: 1-1/2" = 1'-0"   N:\24701_00\DET\6\GR01.DWG

below (reverse clockwise from top left) Product showrooms, and conference
/ opposite page room, at building one, second floor.
/ Product showroom.

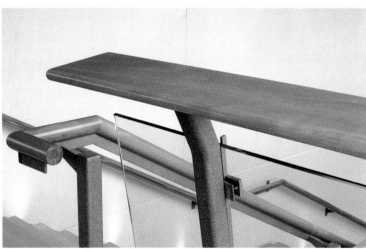

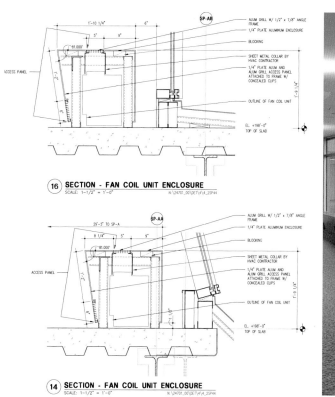

16   **SECTION - FAN COIL UNIT ENCLOSURE**
SCALE: 1-1/2" = 1'-0"

14   **SECTION - FAN COIL UNIT ENCLOSURE**
SCALE: 1-1/2" = 1'-0"

below and opposite page   Running track at Fitness Center, and
construction document of soffit at
skylight. / Spine curtain wall and
running track detail view.

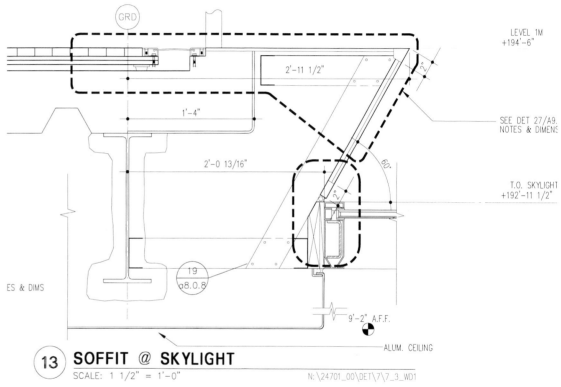

LEVEL 1M
+194'-6"

GRD

2'-11 1/2"

1'-4"

SEE DET 27/A9.
NOTES & DIMENS

2'-0 13/16"

60°

T.O. SKYLIGHT
+192'-11 1/2"

2"

ES & DIMS

19
a8.0.8

9'-2" A.F.F.

ALUM. CEILING

(13) **SOFFIT @ SKYLIGHT**
SCALE: 1 1/2" = 1'-0"   N:\24701_00\DET\7\7_3_WD1

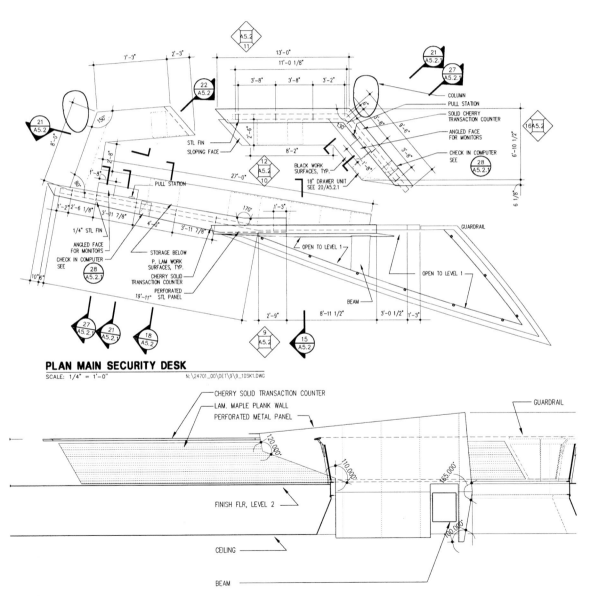

PLAN MAIN SECURITY DESK
SCALE: 1/4" = 1'-0"   N:\24701_00\DET\9\9_1DSK1.DWG

ELEVATION MAIN SECURITY DESK
SCALE: 1/4" = 1'-0"   N:\24701_00\DET\9\9_1DSK1.DWG

below (reverse clockwise from top right) / opposite page

Spine curtain wall, main stair and elevator core wall details. / Curtain wall detail at spine termination.

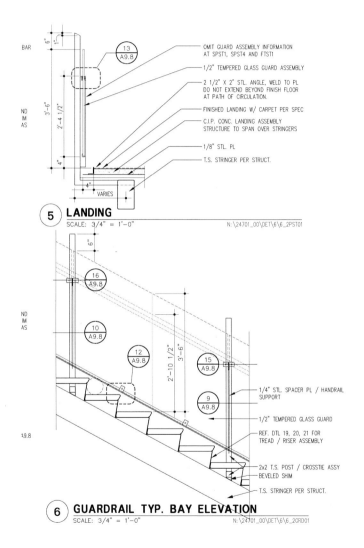

OMIT GUARD ASSEMBLY INFORMATION
AT SPST1, SPST4 AND FTST1

1/2" TEMPERED GLASS GUARD ASSEMBLY

2 1/2" X 2" STL. ANGLE, WELD TO PL
DO NOT EXTEND BEYOND FINISH FLOOR
AT PATH OF CIRCULATION.

FINISHED LANDING W/ CARPET PER SPEC

C.I.P. CONC. LANDING ASSEMBLY
STRUCTURE TO SPAN OVER STRINGERS

1/8" STL. PL

T.S. STRINGER PER STRUCT.

5 **LANDING**
SCALE: 3/4" = 1'-0"   N:\24701_00\DET\6\6_2PST01

1/4" STL. SPACER PL / HANDRAIL
SUPPORT

1/2" TEMPERED GLASS GUARD

REF. DTL 19, 20, 21 FOR
TREAD / RISER ASSEMBLY

2x2 T.S. POST / CROSSTIE ASSY
BEVELED SHIM

T.S. STRINGER PER STRUCT.

6 **GUARDRAIL TYP. BAY ELEVATION**
SCALE: 3/4" = 1'-0"   N:\24701_00\DET\6\6_2GRD01

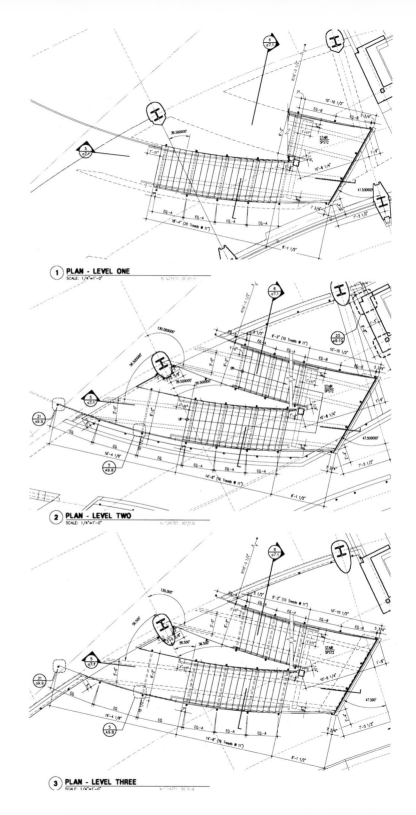

1 PLAN - LEVEL ONE
SCALE: 1/4"=1'-0"

2 PLAN - LEVEL TWO
SCALE: 1/4"=1'-0"

3 PLAN - LEVEL THREE
SCALE: 1/4"=1'-0"

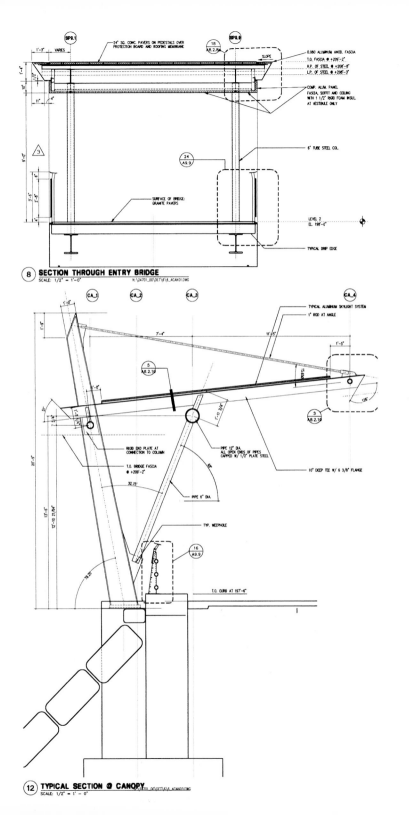

8) SECTION THROUGH ENTRY BRIDGE
SCALE: 1/2" = 1'-0"

24" SQ. CONC. PAVERS ON PEDESTALS OVER
PROTECTION BOARD AND ROOFING MEMBRANE

0.080 ALUMINUM ANOD. FASCIA
T.O. FASCIA @ +209'-2"
H.P. OF STEEL @ +208'-8"
L.P. OF STEEL @ +208'-3"

COMP. ALUM. PANEL
FASCIA, SOFFIT AND CEILING
WITH 1 1/2" RIGID FOAM INSUL.
AT VESTIBULE ONLY

6" TUBE STEEL COL.

SURFACE OF BRIDGE:
GRANITE PAVERS

LEVEL 2
EL. 198'-0"

TYPICAL DRIP EDGE

12) TYPICAL SECTION @ CANOPY
SCALE: 1/2" = 1'-0"

TYPICAL ALUMINUM SKYLIGHT SYSTEM
1" ROD AT ANGLE

RIGID END PLATE AT
CONNECTION TO COLUMN

PIPE 12" DIA.
ALL OPEN ENDS OF PIPES
CAPPED W/ 1/2" PLATE STEEL

T.O. BRIDGE FASCIA
@ +209'-2"

10" DEEP TEE W/ 6 3/8" FLANGE

PIPE 8" DIA.

TYP. WEEPHOLE

T.O. CURB AT 197'-6"

Building two with terrace over cafeteria and dining areas on right. / Building two sloped and vertical curtain wall detail view. / Southwest view.

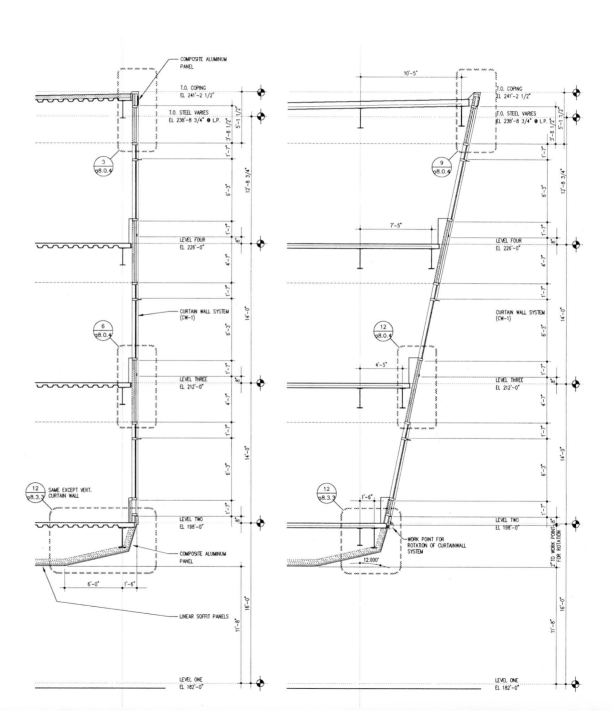

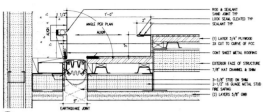

ROD & SEALANT
SAND JOINT TYP
LOCK SEAM, CLEATED TYP
ANGLE PER PLAN
ALIGN
SEALANT TYP
(1) LAYER 3/4" PLYWOOD
2X CUT TO CURVE OF PCC
CONT SHEET METAL ROOFING
EXTERIOR FACE OF STRUCTURE
7/8" HAT CHANNEL & SHIM
3-5/8" STUD ON SHIM
2-1/2" 16 GUAGE METAL STUD
FIRE SAFING
(2) LAYERS 5/8" GWB

EARTHQUAKE JOINT

(1) TYP SPINE TO CORE EXPANSION JOINT
SCALE: 3" = 1'-0"

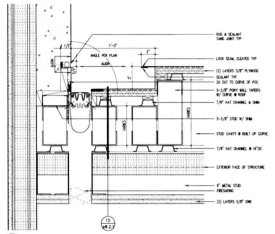

ROD & SEALANT
SAND JOINT TYP
LOCK SEAM, CLEATED TYP
ANGLE PER PLAN
ALIGN
(2) LAYERS 3/8" PLYWOOD
SEALANT TYP
2X CUT TO CURVE OF PCC
3-5/8" PONY WALL TAPERS
W/ CURVE @ ROOF
7/8" HAT CHANNEL & SHIM
3-5/8" STUD W/ SHIM
STUD CAVITY @ BUILT UP CURVE
7/8" HAT CHANNEL @ 16"OC
EXTERIOR FACE OF STRUCTURE
6" METAL STUD
FIRESAFING
(2) LAYERS 5/8" GWB

15
d8.2

(3) TYP SPINE TO CORE REVEAL
SCALE: 3" = 1'-0"

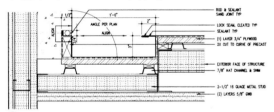

ROD & SEALANT
SAND JOINT TYP
ANGLE PER PLAN
LOCK SEAM, CLEATED TYP
ALIGN
(1) LAYER 3/4" PLYWOOD
2X CUT TO CURVE OF PRECAST
EXTERIOR FACE OF STRUCTURE
7/8" HAT CHANNEL & SHIM
2-1/2" 16 GUAGE METAL STUD
(2) LAYERS 5/8" GWB

(4) TYP SPINE TO CORE REVEAL
SCALE: 3" = 1'-0"

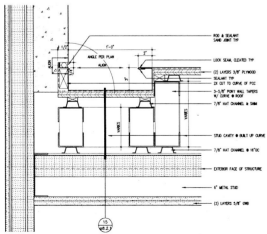

ROD & SEALANT
SAND JOINT TYP
ANGLE PER PLAN
LOCK SEAM, CLEATED TYP
ALIGN
(2) LAYERS 3/8" PLYWOOD
SEALANT TYP
2X CUT TO CURVE OF PCC
3-5/8" PONY WALL TAPERS
W/ CURVE @ ROOF
7/8" HAT CHANNEL & SHIM
STUD CAVITY @ BUILT UP CURVE
7/8" HAT CHANNEL @ 16"OC
EXTERIOR FACE OF STRUCTURE
6" METAL STUD
(2) LAYERS 5/8" GWB

15
d8.2

(6) TYP SPINE TO CORE REVEAL
SCALE: 3" = 1'-0"

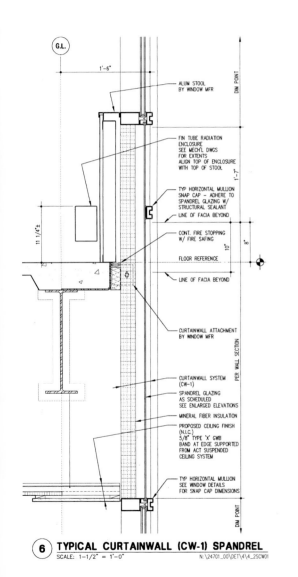

6 **TYPICAL CURTAINWALL (CW-1) SPANDREL**
SCALE: 1-1/2" = 1'-0"   N:\24701_00\DET\4\4_2SCW01

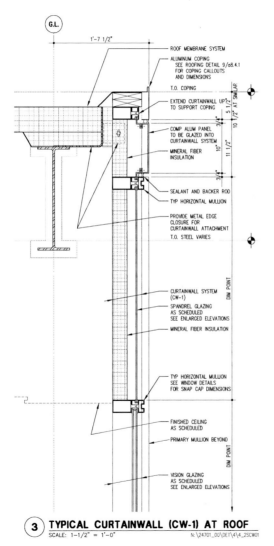

3 **TYPICAL CURTAINWALL (CW-1) AT ROOF**
SCALE: 1-1/2" = 1'-0"   N:\24701_00\DET\4\4_2SCW01

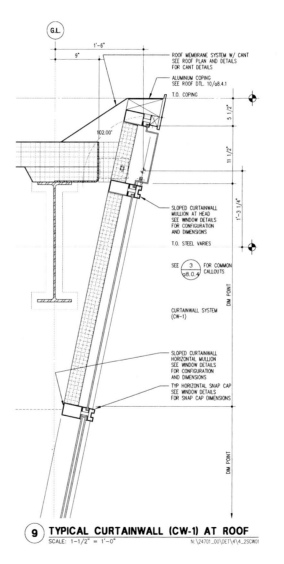

9 **TYPICAL CURTAINWALL (CW-1) AT ROOF**
SCALE: 1-1/2" = 1'-0"   N:\24701_00\DET\4\4_2SCW01

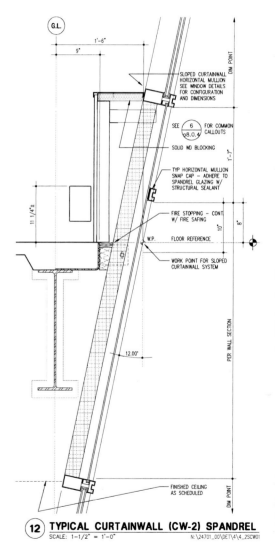

12 **TYPICAL CURTAINWALL (CW-2) SPANDREL**
SCALE: 1-1/2" = 1'-0"   N:\24701_00\DET\4\4_2SCW01

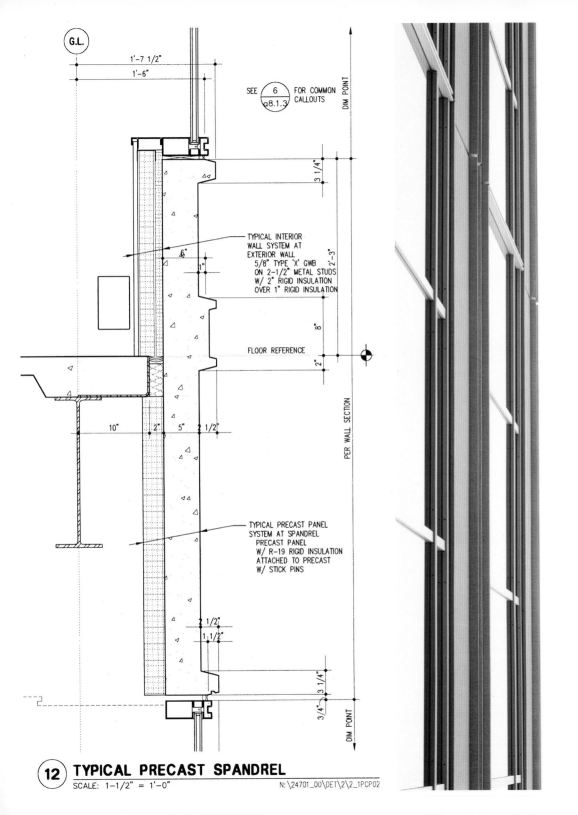

1'-7 1/2"

1'-6"

SEE 6 FOR COMMON CALLOUTS
a8.1.3

DIM POINT

3 1/4"

TYPICAL INTERIOR WALL SYSTEM AT EXTERIOR WALL
5/8" TYPE 'X' GWB ON 2-1/2" METAL STUDS W/ 2" RIGID INSULATION OVER 1" RIGID INSULATION

6"

1"

2'-3"

8"

FLOOR REFERENCE

2"

PER WALL SECTION

10"   2"   5"   2 1/2"

TYPICAL PRECAST PANEL SYSTEM AT SPANDREL
PRECAST PANEL W/ R-19 RIGID INSULATION ATTACHED TO PRECAST W/ STICK PINS

2 1/2"

1 1/2"

3 1/4"

3/4"

DIM POINT

12 TYPICAL PRECAST SPANDREL

SCALE: 1-1/2" = 1'-0"

N:\24701_00\DET\2\2_1PCP02

below (clockwise from top left) / opposite page

Fitness Center: projected roof, curtain wall, and stairway projection; building three: window wall, service wall, and curtain wall. / Building three window wall working drawing detail and view of Fitness Center projected roof.

below / opposite page   Running truck tunnel at Fitness Center.
/ Fitness Center between buildings
three and four.

below (clockwise from top left) /
opposite page

Building four: window wall detail view;
curtain wall detail view; sofit construction
documents; sofit corner detail view; and
curtain wall detail view. / Fitness Center
stairway projection.

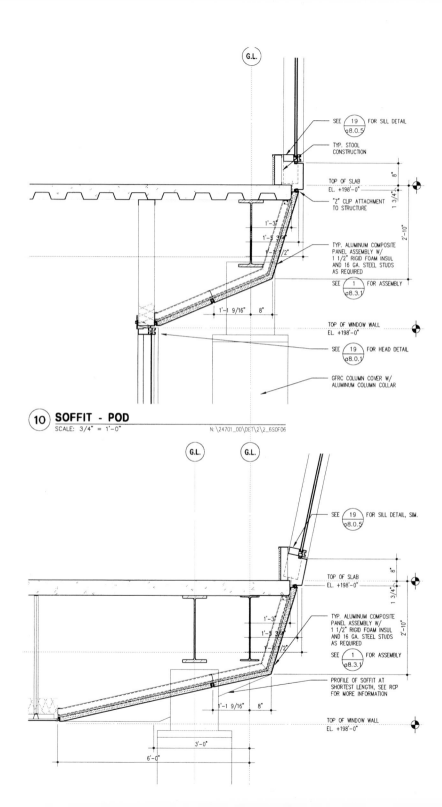

SEE 19 FOR SILL DETAIL
a8.0.5

TYP. STOOL
CONSTRUCTION

TOP OF SLAB
EL. +198'-0"

"Z" CLIP ATTACHMENT
TO STRUCTURE

TYP. ALUMINUM COMPOSITE
PANEL ASSEMBLY W/
1 1/2" RIGID FOAM INSUL
AND 16 GA. STEEL STUDS
AS REQUIRED

SEE 1 FOR ASSEMBLY
a8.3.1

TOP OF WINDOW WALL
EL. +198'-0"

SEE 19 FOR HEAD DETAIL
a8.0.1

GFRC COLUMN COVER W/
ALUMINUM COLUMN COLLAR

10 SOFFIT - POD
SCALE: 3/4" = 1'-0"
N:\24701_00\DET\2\2_6SOF06

SEE 19 FOR SILL DETAIL, SIM.
a8.0.5

TOP OF SLAB
EL. +198'-0"

TYP. ALUMINUM COMPOSITE
PANEL ASSEMBLY W/
1 1/2" RIGID FOAM INSUL
AND 16 GA. STEEL STUDS
AS REQUIRED

SEE 1 FOR ASSEMBLY
a8.3.1

PROFILE OF SOFFIT AT
SHORTEST LENGTH, SEE RCP
FOR MORE INFORMATION

TOP OF WINDOW WALL
EL. +198'-0"

VISION GLAZING
AS SCHEDULED
SEE ENLARGED ELEVATIONS

ALUM STOOL
BY WINDOW MFR

TYP HORIZONTAL MULLION

SPANDREL GLAZING
AS SCHEDULED

FIN TUBE RADIATION
ENCLOSURE

TYPICAL INTERIOR
WALL SYSTEM AT
EXTERIOR WALL
5/8" TYPE 'X' GWB
ON 2-1/2" METAL STUDS
W/ 2" RIGID INSULATION
OVER 1" RIGID INSULATION

TYPICAL SILL
SEE WINDOW DETAILS
FOR SNAP CAP DIMENSIONS

FIRE STOPPING - CONT
W/ FIRE SAFING

FLOOR REFERENCE

LOCATION OF
WINDOW MULLION
AT CURTAINWALL
SEE
2
28.0.4

FLUTED PRECAST
PANEL

PROPOSED CEILING FINISH
(N.I.C.)
5/8" TYPE 'X' GWB
BAND AT EDGE SUPPORTED
FROM ACT SUSPENDED
CEILING SYSTEM

TYP HORIZONTAL HEAD
SEE WINDOW DETAILS
FOR SNAP CAP DIMENSIONS

G.L.

1'-7 1/2"
1'-6"

WINDOW DIM POINT

1'-7"

11 1/4"±

10"

8"

10"   2"   7 1/2"

2 1/2"

3'-5"

PER WALL SECTION

13 FLUTES @ 3" O.C. = 3'-0"

2 1/2"

4"

DIM POINT

6 **TYPICAL FLUTED PRECAST SPANDREL**
SCALE: 1-1/2" = 1'-0"   N:\24701_00\DET\2\2_1PCP02

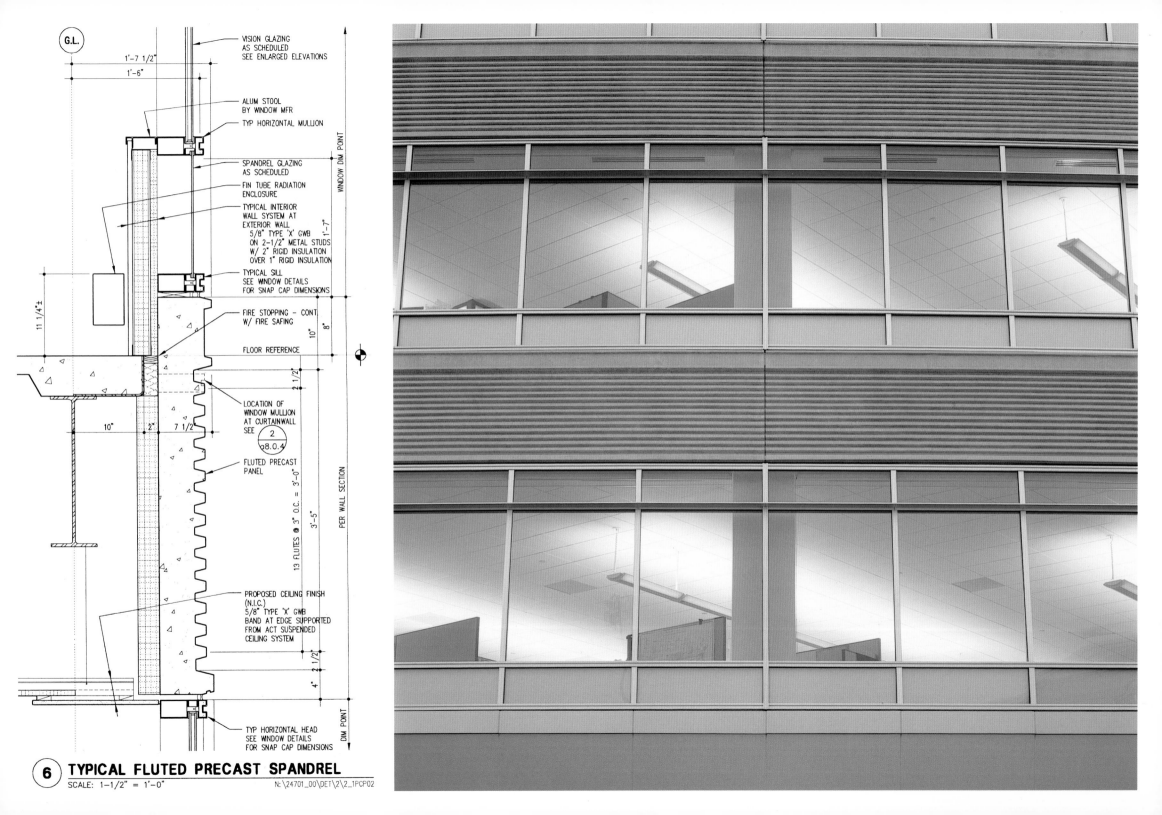

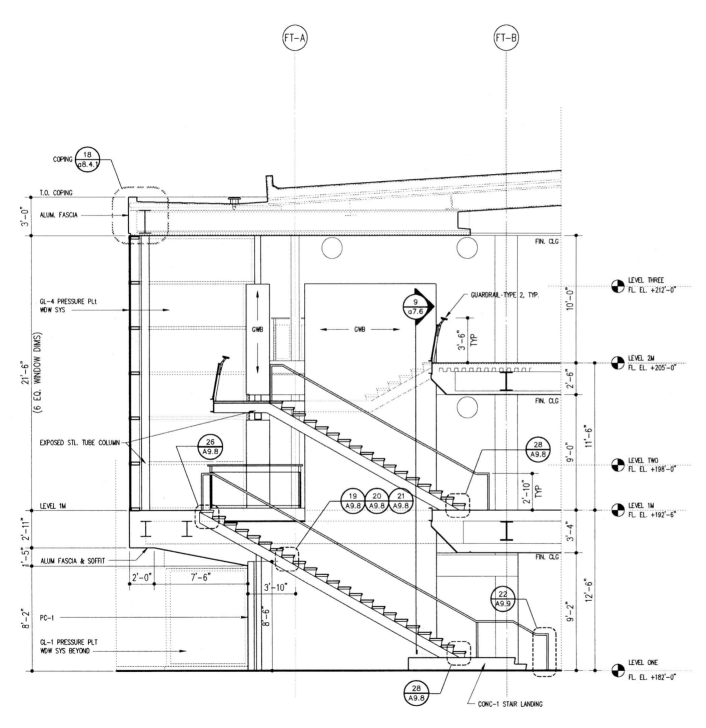

COPING ⌾18/8.4.1

T.O. COPING

ALUM. FASCIA

3'-0"

GL-4 PRESSURE PLt WDW SYS

21'-6" (6 EQ. WINDOW DIMS)

GWB

GWB

GWB

GUARDRAIL-TYPE 2, TYP.

⌾9/7.6

3'-6" TYP

FIN. CLG

LEVEL THREE FL. EL. +212'-0"

10'-0"

LEVEL 2M FL. EL. +205'-0"

2'-6"

FIN. CLG

EXPOSED STL. TUBE COLUMN

⌾26/A9.8

⌾28/A9.8

11'-6"

9'-0"

LEVEL TWO FL. EL. +198'-0"

LEVEL 1M

⌾19/A9.8 ⌾20/A9.8 ⌾21/A9.8

2'-10" TYP

LEVEL 1M FL. EL. +192'-6"

2'-11"

3'-4"

FIN. CLG

1'-5"

ALUM FASCIA & SOFFIT

2'-0"

7'-6"

3'-10"

8'-6"

⌾22/A9.9

12'-6"

9'-2"

8'-2"

PC-1

GL-1 PRESSURE PLT WDW SYS BEYOND

LEVEL ONE FL. EL. +182'-0"

⌾28/A9.8

CONC-1 STAIR LANDING

FT-A   FT-B

⑥ **SECTION FTST1**
SCALE: 1/4" = 1'-0"   N:\24701_00\DWG\A7_6.DWG

below / opposite page   Spine termination at building four stair.
/   Construction document and exterior
view of stair at building four.

below / opposite page / following spread Canopy at main entrance. / Spine termination glazing detail. / Curtain wall views at spine from southeast.

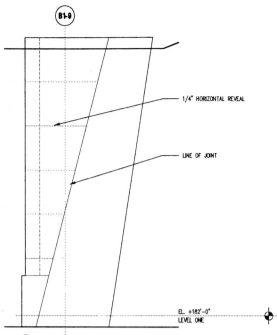

1/4" HORIZONTAL REVEAL

LINE OF JOINT

EL +182'-0"
LEVEL ONE

16 ELEV GFRC COL COVER - BUILDING ONE
SCALE: 1/2" = 1'-0"   N:\24701_00\DET\2\2_1GFR02

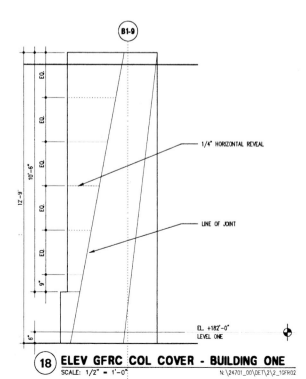

1/4" HORIZONTAL REVEAL

LINE OF JOINT

EL +182'-0"
LEVEL ONE

18 ELEV GFRC COL COVER - BUILDING ONE
SCALE: 1/2" = 1'-0"   N:\24701_00\DET\2\2_1GFR02

below / opposite page   Curtain wall detail at spine elevation.
                        / Curving ramp to entrance with
                        building one on the right.

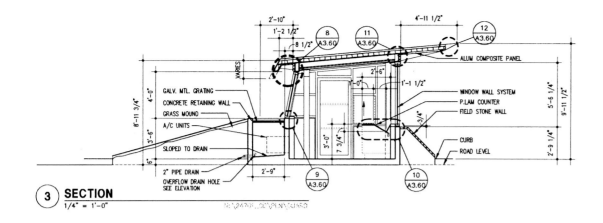

3 SECTION
1/4" = 1'-0"

Labels (section 3, top):
2'-10"
1'-2 1/2"
8 1/2"
4'-11 1/2"
8 A3.60
11 A3.60
12 A3.60
ALUM COMPOSITE PANEL
VARIES
GALV. MTL. GRATING
CONCRETE RETAINING WALL
GRASS MOUND
A/C UNITS
SLOPED TO DRAIN
2" PIPE DRAIN
OVERFLOW DRAIN HOLE SEE ELEVATION
2'-9"
3'-0"
7 3/4"
1'-0"
2'-6"
1'-1 1/2"
3/4"
WINDOW WALL SYSTEM
P.LAM COUNTER
FIELD STONE WALL
CURB
ROAD LEVEL
9 A3.60
10 A3.60
8'-11 3/4"
4'-0"
3'-6"
6"
5'-6 1/4"
9'-11 1/2"
2'-9 1/4"

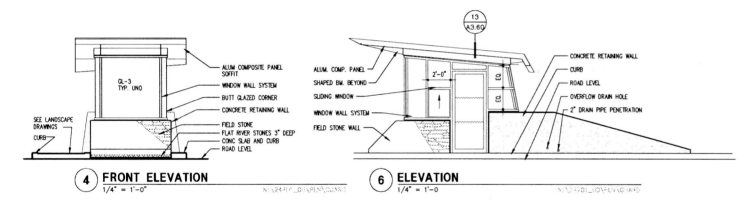

4 FRONT ELEVATION
1/4" = 1'-0"

GL-3 TYP. UNO
SEE LANDSCAPE DRAWINGS
CURB
ALUM COMPOSITE PANEL SOFFIT
WINDOW WALL SYSTEM
BUTT GLAZED CORNER
CONCRETE RETAINING WALL
FIELD STONE
FLAT RIVER STONES 3" DEEP
CONC SLAB AND CURB
ROAD LEVEL

6 ELEVATION
1/4" = 1'-0

13 A3.60
ALUM. COMP. PANEL
SHAPED BM. BEYOND
SLIDING WINDOW
WINDOW WALL SYSTEM
FIELD STONE WALL
2'-0"
EQ
EQ
CONCRETE RETAINING WALL
CURB
ROAD LEVEL
OVERFLOW DRAIN HOLE
2" DRAIN PIPE PENETRATION

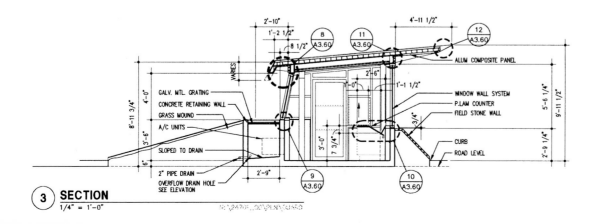

3 SECTION
1/4" = 1'-0"

Labels (section 3, bottom):
2'-10"
1'-2 1/2"
8 1/2"
4'-11 1/2"
8 A3.60
11 A3.60
12 A3.60
ALUM COMPOSITE PANEL
VARIES
GALV. MTL. GRATING
CONCRETE RETAINING WALL
GRASS MOUND
A/C UNITS
SLOPED TO DRAIN
2" PIPE DRAIN
OVERFLOW DRAIN HOLE SEE ELEVATION
2'-9"
3'-0"
7 3/4"
1'-0"
2'-6"
1'-1 1/2"
3/4"
WINDOW WALL SYSTEM
P.LAM COUNTER
FIELD STONE WALL
CURB
ROAD LEVEL
9 A3.60
10 A3.60
8'-11 3/4"
4'-0"
3'-6"
6"
5'-6 1/4"
9'-11 1/2"
2'-9 1/4"

one thirteen realization

below / opposite page Ramp leading to main entrance. /
Construction documents and side
view of south entrance gate house.

one zero nine realization

Reebok World Headquarters in context. / North entrance gate house with complex beyond. / Complex north entry view.

On August 15th 2001, NBBJ's leading designers responsible for Reebok gathered to discuss the project. The designers include Scott Wyatt, Steven McConnell, Rob Swartz, Jonathan Ward, Nick Charles, Ruben Gonzalez, Jin Ah Park, Chris Larson, and Rick Buckley. Their commentary follows: ■ Paul Fireman knew that Reebok could not be average or even above average. Reebok had to be extraordinary. ■ The opportunity was wide open to synthesize Reebok's varied views about who they were. ■ Our job was to design creative spaces with purpose. We recognized that Reebok has many components yet functions as a cohesive whole—as One. ■ They were not able to visualize how space could translate into who they are, however they knew they needed to move, literally and figuratively. As designers, we were able to come up with a vision, and make it a reality. ■ Reebok's lease was expiring. The company could renew, move, or build new. The cost of starting new was comparable to the other options, but Paul Fireman wanted more. He wanted to add value to the company. ■ We found the design heart and soul of the business with the creative staff. The notion of performance design implies continual development and change to achieve a better product. This means content rich work, informed and inspired by ideas. ■ From the perspective of interiors, our big breakthrough was to get the venues for sports and fitness integrated into the fabric of the building so that you could see, hear and feel the application of the products from within the headquarters. ■ We put the fitness center into the heart of the spine. Instead of being compartmentalized, the business of sports and fitness became integrated. ■ The building

creates a synergy between the interior and the exterior. Views of the athletic fields connect the employees with the purpose of their work and, from outside, the glass reflects the running track, becoming a mirror for activities that drive Reebok's business. ■ There is no second-class space. The building is designed for good views in all directions. Everyone has equal access. ■ The showrooms are not compartmentalized. Satellite spaces are exposed to major circulation and keep the products visible. ■ The showrooms can serve as office space. They are asymmetrical so that each has its own unique feel and personality. ■ The inspiration for the interiors was to make them transformational. We took an organic approach to space, literally thinking out of the box. The rooms do not have a cubic nature, but rather are dynamic—more suited to the way in which humans relate to space. ■ The asymmetrical nature of the spaces meant that more drawings were required for the builders. However, the complexity of the design added to the ultimate value of the project. ■ The onus was on us to figure out how to describe the design, to define a process and document it. The project was as transformational for NBBJ as for Reebok. ■ This project marked the first time we attached multiple sets of 3-D drawings. ■ The design and documentation process was compressed within the eight month schedule. To expedite the work, we kept the original competition digital model and simply continued adding to it. The contractor pinned the model sheets on the walls where daily meetings were held to aid visualization of the building. ■ We brought the project along incrementally, massaging the design and making it more real each

day. We offered the client more than they had asked for. ■ The process was suited to the anthropomorphic nature of the project inspired by the runner. We found ourselves using terms such as spine, movement and action to explain issues. ■ The use of contrasting materials—rubber, steel, pre-cast, glass, plaster—creates a sense of action. ■ The organization of the design has an organic intelligence. Reebok is not a box. ■ The concept for the building is dramatic and powerful. The space simply opens up to the views. ■ We wanted to activate the spine. One solution was to locate the elevator cores at the spine, away from the center of the office pods. The resulting circulation flow enlivens the spine and creates opportunities for serendipitous interaction. ■ Within the spine anything having to do with moving people around is expressed and brought out into the open. The elevators are exposed vertical towers, the stairs are sculptural, the running track comes right into the building. The spine is an urban scene with people moving along various expressways. ■ We created a variety of spaces, both public and private. We were inspired by how Reebok does work. ■ We wanted to offer Reebok's workforce a space with life and vitality. By connecting people to the essence of sports and fitness activities we achieved an enviroment that offers outrageous motivation. ■ In building this project, we communicated with the entire team, always finding a solution, and making it more real each day. ■ We took ideas and made them real. We took something that was inherently complex and broke it down into parts that made sense. The key was to think on a grand scale. ■ All the materials are familiar, such as precast concrete and steel.

■ The Reebok World Headquarters is an example of transformational architecture, bringing a vision into reality, and making it a functional workspace. ■ The beauty of the building is that we were able to hide the working guts, keeping that aspect of the project unobtrusive. For example the central plant and service distribution are hidden in the basement. ■ It is a functional building with many complex systems that allow for comfort, ensuring fresh air and warmth. ■ The core was pulled out of the center of each office pod leaving a 30,000-square-foot footprint for open office. ■ For the eight days of the competition, we put together a team of highly talented people, formed mini-charrettes, and held several discussions each day. Every day was an opportunity for finding another way of looking at things. ■ The design team kept the same kind of spirit throughout the job. The process that we followed during the competition is now legendary. The key was to focus on the most important things, because there was simply no time for anything else. ■ There was commitment to the concept from everyone on the team; everyone owned a bit of the design. In other words, the sum of the parts was greater than the whole. Everyone made a valuable contribution. There was no template, only ideas and rich dialogue. ■ The competition team was an example of collaboration at its best: everyone had control; no one had control. It was the opposite of a linear progression where details are added along the way. Simultaneous creation occurred. Several different groups developed ideas independently which were then plugged back together. ■ The focus was on Reebok, discovering their vision and goals, and finding ways to express them.

■ We got away from the traditional notion of context as the form-giver. The company and its spirit became the context. ■ This design process has longevity. Architects tend to design based on constraints and solving problems. This concept was based solely on developing an idea. An idea does not become a limitation; it generates creativity. ■ The desire was to explore and stay in the world of ideas, using 3-D design tools and true collaboration. Decisions were based on the success of an idea, not on its owner. ■ Throughout the entire project, we pursued Reebok's goals. The new headquarters is for and about Reebok, not the architects.

realization

Aerial photographic sequence of construction: June, July and October 1998; and January, February and March 1999.

january 5   2000 ▶

november 24 **1999** ▶

february 4 **2000** ▶

march 20 **2000** ▶

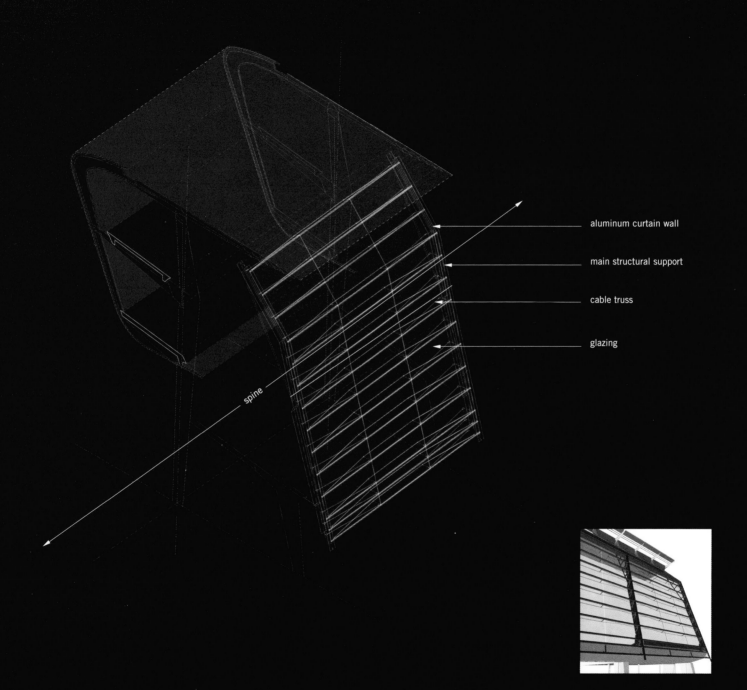

aluminum curtain wall

main structural support

cable truss

glazing

spine

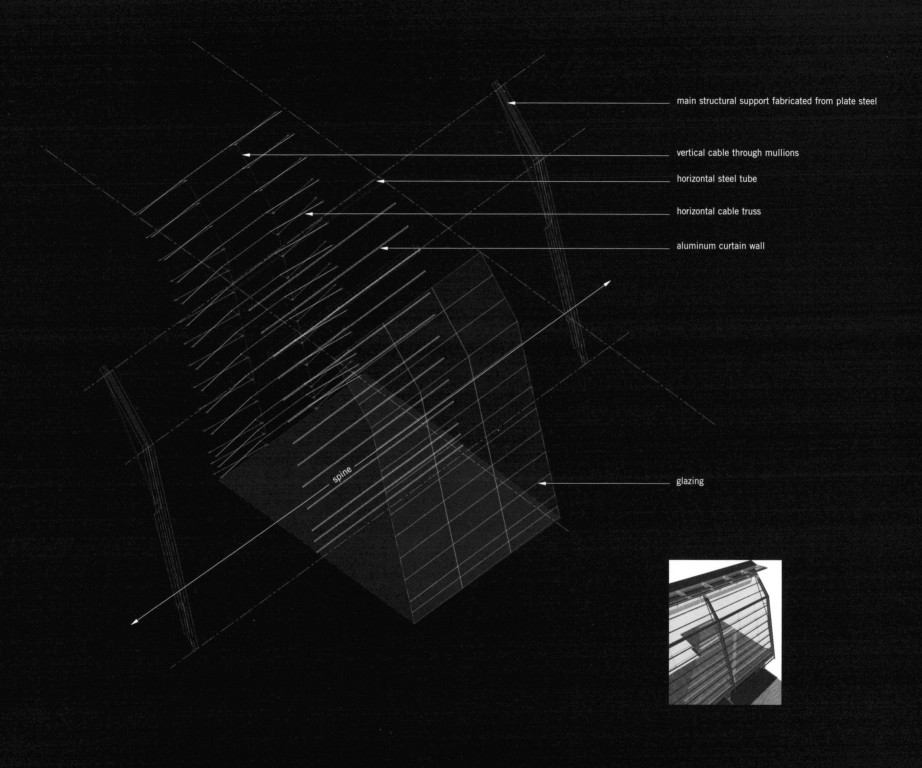

main structural support fabricated from plate steel

vertical cable through mullions

horizontal steel tube

horizontal cable truss

aluminum curtain wall

glazing

spine

september 9 **1999** ▶

october 29 **1999** ▶

august 16 1999 ▶

october 8 1999 ▶

june 20 1999 ▶

july 20 1999 ▶

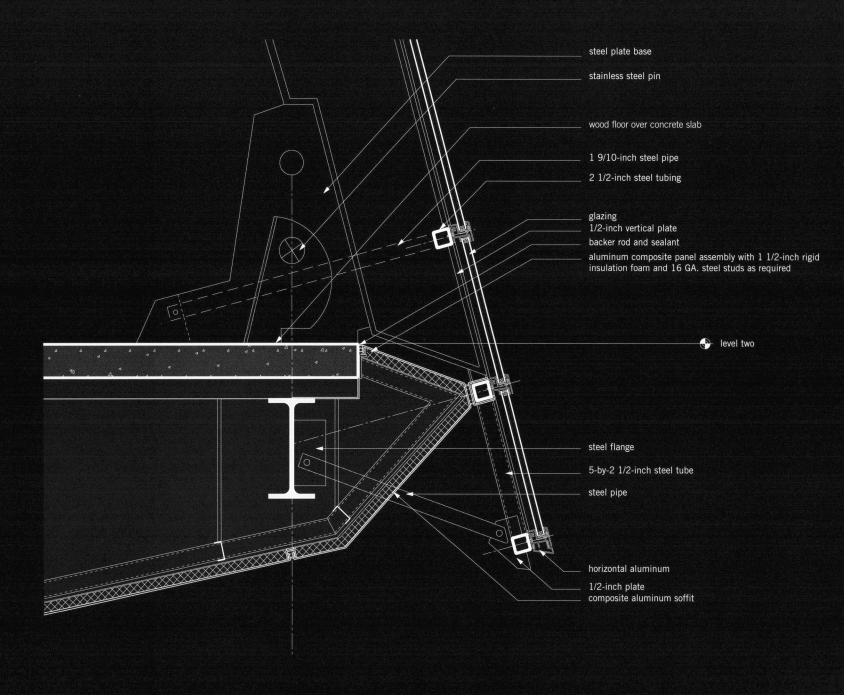

below   Detail of spine curtainwall connection at level two.

steel plate base

stainless steel pin

wood floor over concrete slab

1 9/10-inch steel pipe

2 1/2-inch steel tubing

glazing
1/2-inch vertical plate
backer rod and sealant
aluminum composite panel assembly with 1 1/2-inch rigid
insulation foam and 16 GA. steel studs as required

level two

steel flange

5-by-2 1/2-inch steel tube

steel pipe

horizontal aluminum

1/2-inch plate
composite aluminum soffit

april 29 1999 ►

april 12 1999 ▶

may 25 1999 ▶

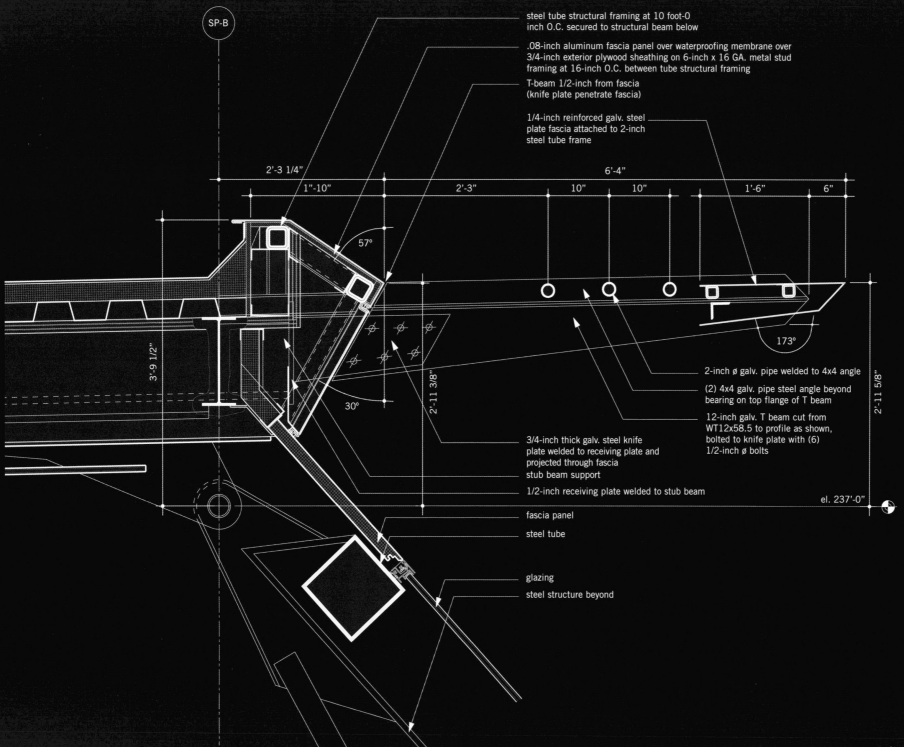

SP-B

steel tube structural framing at 10 foot-0
inch O.C. secured to structural beam below

.08-inch aluminum fascia panel over waterproofing membrane over
3/4-inch exterior plywood sheathing on 6-inch x 16 GA. metal stud
framing at 16-inch O.C. between tube structural framing

T-beam 1/2-inch from fascia
(knife plate penetrate fascia)

1/4-inch reinforced galv. steel
plate fascia attached to 2-inch
steel tube frame

2'-3 1/4"

6'-4"

1"-10"

2'-3"

10"

10"

1'-6"

6"

57°

3'-9 1/2"

30°

2'-11 3/8"

173°

2'-11 5/8"

2-inch ø galv. pipe welded to 4x4 angle

(2) 4x4 galv. pipe steel angle beyond
bearing on top flange of T beam

12-inch galv. T beam cut from
WT12x58.5 to profile as shown,
bolted to knife plate with (6)
1/2-inch ø bolts

3/4-inch thick galv. steel knife
plate welded to receiving plate and
projected through fascia
stub beam support

1/2-inch receiving plate welded to stub beam

el. 237'-0"

fascia panel

steel tube

glazing

steel structure beyond

april 7 1999 ▶

november 6 1998 ▶

march 5 1999 ▶

july 31 **1998** ▶

february 19 **1999** ▶

april 2 **1999** ▶

Seeing Reebok World Headquarters emerge from the grassy fields in Canton, Massachusetts, one senses the inspiration for the design in the image of a sprinter coiled at the starting line. The building's solid concrete base reaches upward and forward into a four-story expanse of glass that appears to float free of gravity into the future. ■ To capture the essence of action, the building incorporates curves and angles with construction challenges not encountered in standard rectangular buildings. The 350-foot-long circulation spine's tension cable system supports a 40-foot-high wall of glass that curves in segments and tilts at 15- to 43-degree angles. This vast amount of glass, coupled with an intricate horizontal tension truss system, creates a nearly seamless division between the structure's interior and exterior. Unlike most curtain walls, where large aluminum mullions separate the succession of glass panes, the use of slender tubular steel bracing avoids disruptions in the spine's panoramic views of the nearby track, soccer and baseball fields, and tennis courts. ■ Due to the project's size, complex design, and aggressive 23-month delivery schedule, the Canton-based construction firm of O'Connor Constructors formed a joint venture with Turner Construction Company. NBBJ's computer models enabled the field engineers to map over 5,000 survey points to lay out the building, greatly facilitating the process, but also prompting the builders to ask the architects, in jest, "What have you got against 90-degree angles?" ■ The tight schedule for the project required a fast-track approach in which the designers, engineers and client worked hand in hand to find solutions and resolve barriers in a highly productive and collaborative way. Doug Noonan, Reebok's director of corporate real estate, directed the building's design and construction, ensuring that the process was cohesive. Ruben Gonzales, NBBJ's lead construction administrator, also remained on site for the duration of construction. ■ "Being on-site was part of a tremendous team effort," observes Gonzales. "Whenever issues arose, I could respond quickly and collaborate directly with the owner. We were able to incorporate the contractor's ideas and suggestions at the moment we determined an opportunity." Although the building ran the construction team through a gauntlet of innovations, the novelty of the structure inspired workers to engage in an experience unlike any other they had encountered. "They were given the opportunity to step out of their comfort zone and create a landmark," Gonzales notes. "Everyone was in awe of the project, because they had never done anything like it. The design inspired dedication and pride, whether pouring concrete or managing the entire project." ■ The active engagement of client, designers and contractors produced new options as construction progressed. For example, 200-year-old granite foundation blocks recovered from Boston's Big Dig were opportunistically purchased at a relatively low cost. These granite blocks now form the sloped retaining wall that parallels the glass spine, replacing the more mundane precast panels originally envisioned. ■ The campus stands as an unusual blend of synthetic features interwoven with the natural environment, and breaks with tradition by emphasizing acres of athletic fields rather than expansive asphalt parking lots. To handle the cars of employees and visitors, two four-level garages were constructed to consolidate approximately 1,450 vehicles, giving clear preference to a variety of sporting activities and preservation of the rural setting. ■ The inspiration to achieve excellence was felt throughout every facet and stage of the construction process. Gonzales reflects on his experience with the team: "I believe the crew was proud to say 'I worked on Reebok.' And this pride was consistent. Everyone worked together without the hierarchal divisions normally present at work sites."

building

below / opposite page   Building section/elevation through
                        fitness center and spine. / Partial
                        building section through spine.

1. spine
2. fitness center
3. entry plinth
4. running track
5. service area
6. elevation - building three

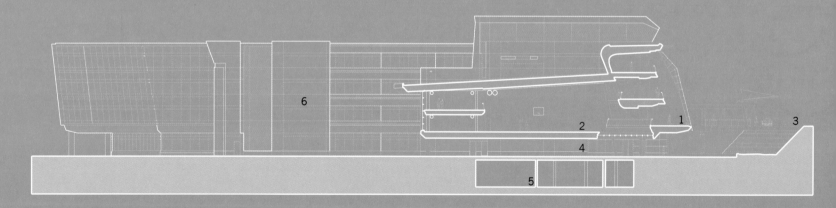

0   20   40ft

1. spine - level four
2. spine - level three
3. fitness center
4. spine - level two
5. running track
6. granite wall
7. storage
8. passage

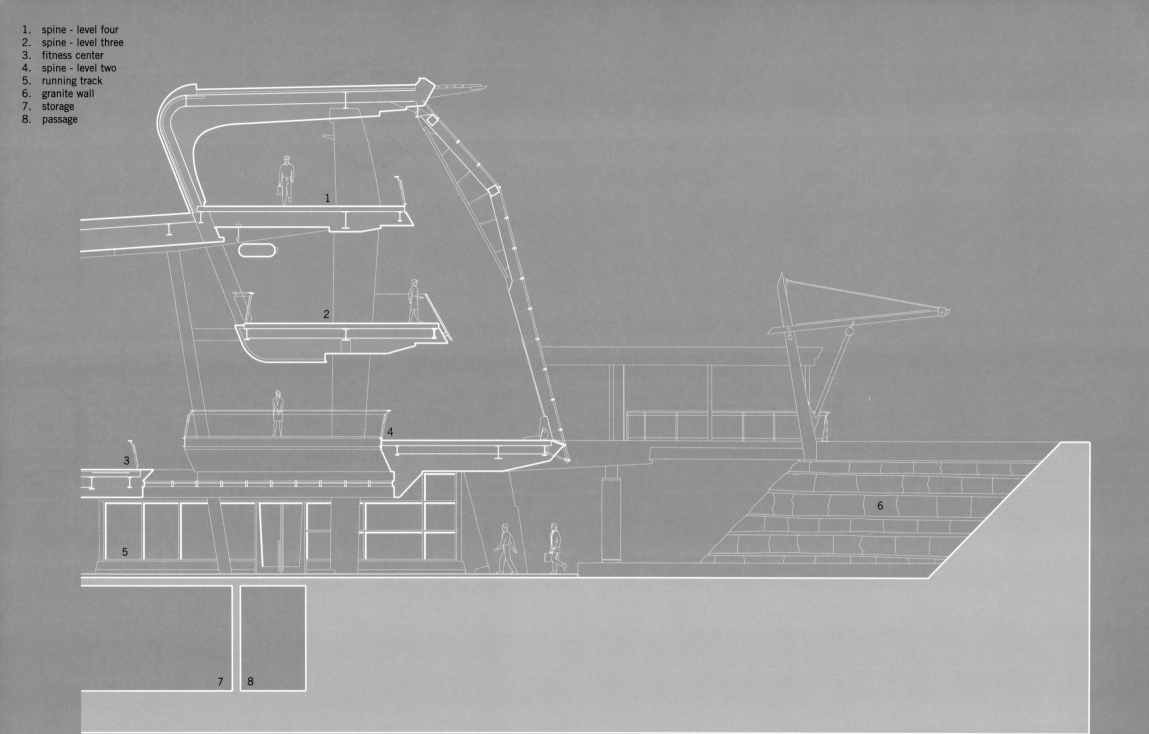

eighty four   process

0   5   10ft

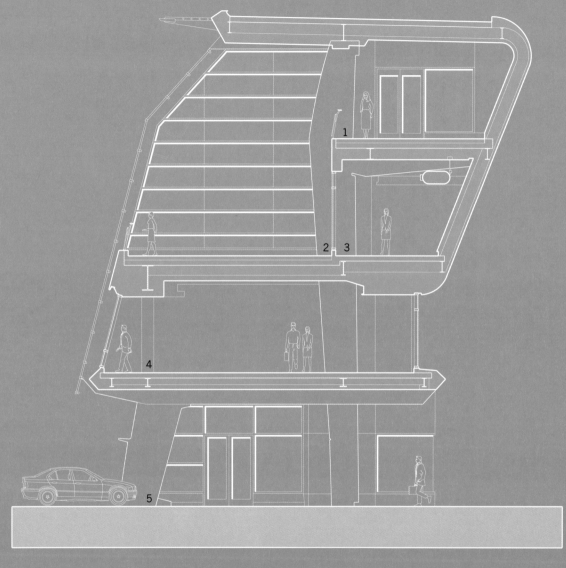

1. terrace - level four
2. terrace - level three
3. corridor
4. spine - level two
5. drive through

0   5   10ft

eighty three   process

1. terrace
2. spine - level two
3. drive through
4. elevation - building two

below / opposite page   Building section/elevation through
spine. / Partial building section
through spine.

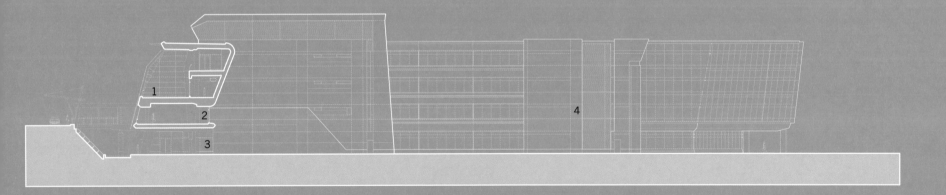

0   20   40ft

below / opposite page Building section/elevation through
spine. / Partial building section
through entry and spine.

1. spine
2. roof terrace
3. entry plinth
4. cafeteria
5. service area
6. elevation - building three

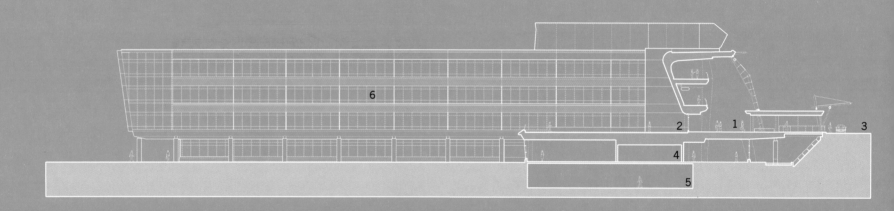

0 20   40ft

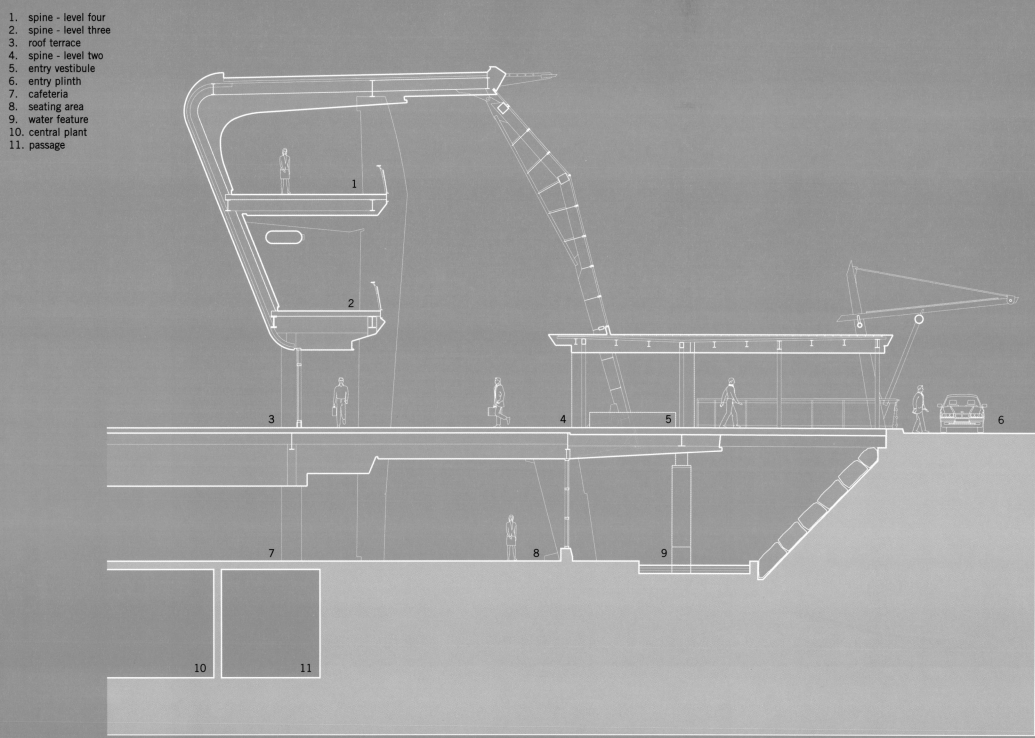

1. spine - level four
2. spine - level three
3. roof terrace
4. spine - level two
5. entry vestibule
6. entry plinth
7. cafeteria
8. seating area
9. water feature
10. central plant
11. passage

eighty process

0   5   10ft

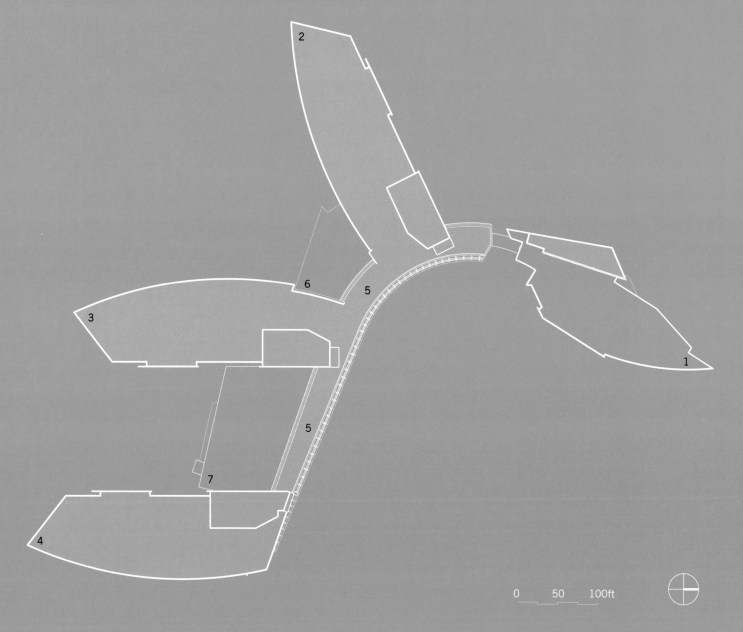

1. building one roof below
2. building two roof
3. building three roof
4. building four roof
5. spine roof
6. cafeteria roof terrace below
7. fitness center roof below

1. building one roof
2. building two shell
3. building three
4. building four
5. spine
6. terrace above drive through
7. fitness center roof
8. building one penthouse

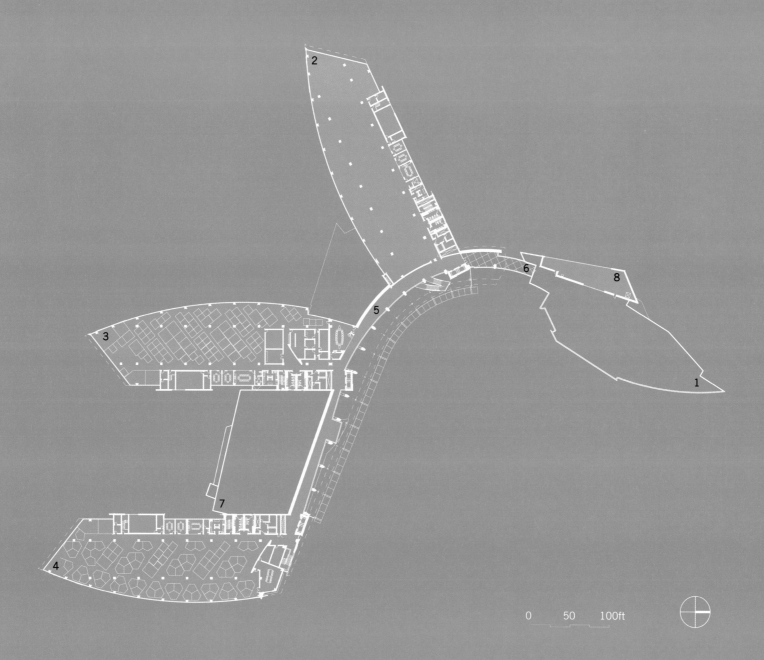

0   50   100ft

1. building one
2. building two
3. building three
4. building four
5. spine
6. main entrance canopy below
7. fitness center mezzanine
8. terrace above drive through

0   50   100ft

1. building one
2. building two
3. building three
4. building four
5. spine
6. exterior terrace
7. fitness center
8. main entrance

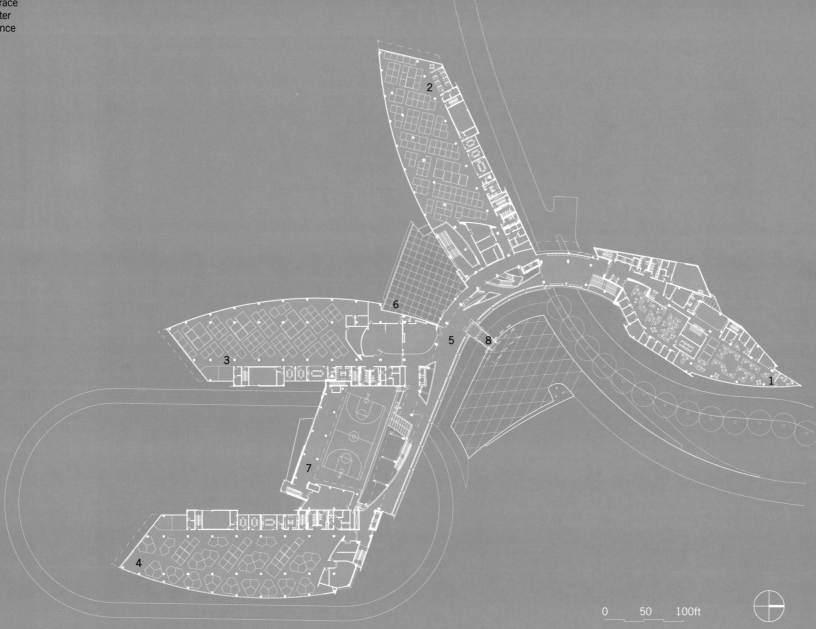

1. building one
2. building two
3. building three
4. building four
5. spine
6. seating area
7. fitness center
8. loading dock below
9. drive through to parking
10. water feature
11. existing manor house
12. cafeteria
13. kitchen
14. conference center
15. product testing laboratory

0   50   100ft

1. shipping and receiving
2. loading dock
3. central plant
4. kitchen
5. storage
6. prototypical model shop
7. computer center

below / opposite page   Subterranean service level plan. / Level one plan.

0   50   100ft

1. corporate headquarters
2. child care center (unbuilt)
3. existing manor house
   (corporate guest house)
4. parking garage
5. subterranean service yard
6. entrance gate house
7. storm water retention pond

0   125   250ft

seventy three process

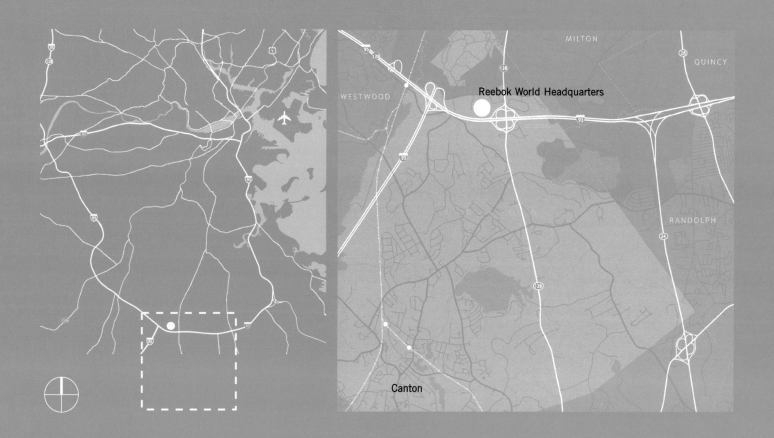

Reebok World Headquarters

below / opposite page   Schematic design of spine termination
at drive through.   /   Schematic design
of exterior spine.

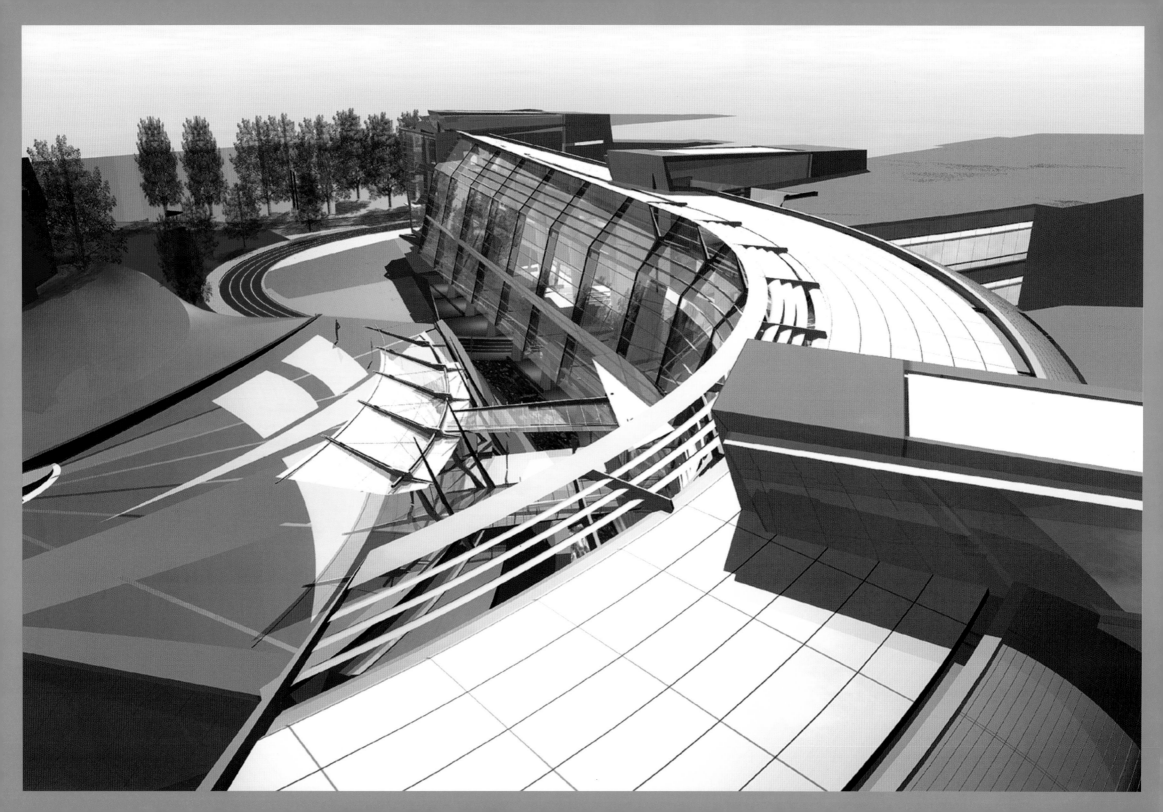

below (clockwise from top left) /
opposite page

Final design of: spine curtain wall termination; spine termination at level three terrace; spine termination at level four terrace; spine bridge aerial view; spine bridge at building one core; and spine bridge ground level view. / Schematic design of spine termination at level four terrace.

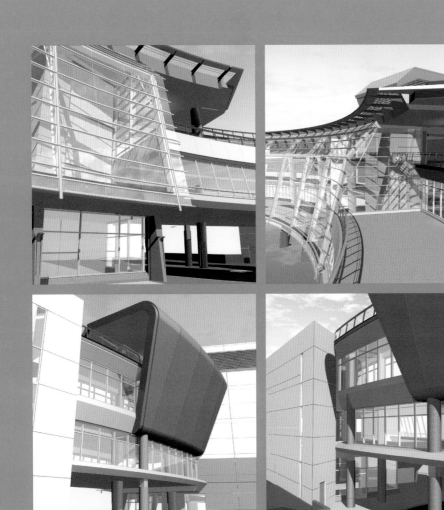

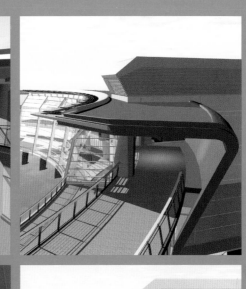

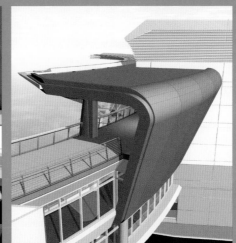

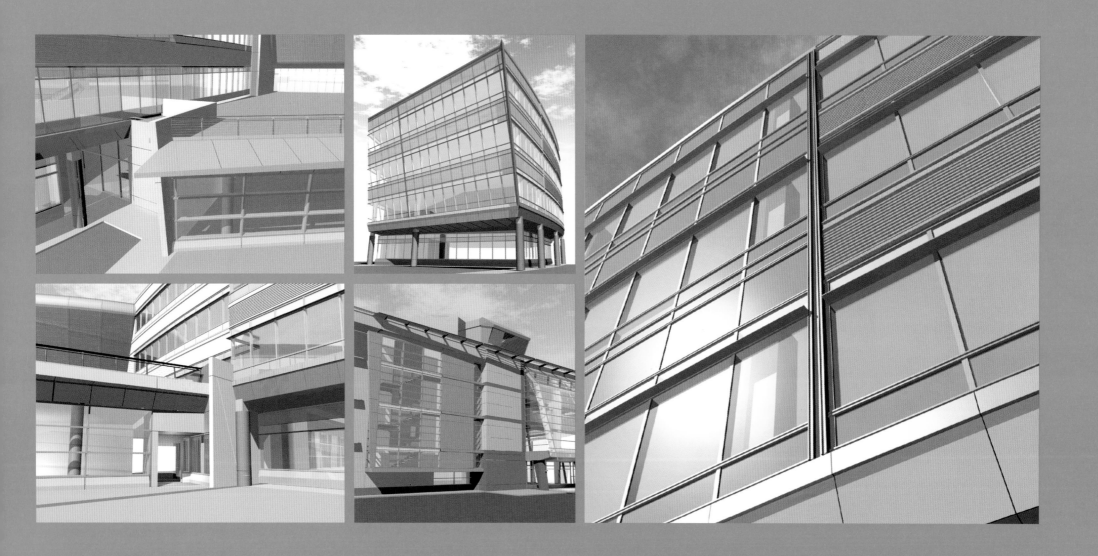

Final design of: sloped glass curtain wall
at eyebrow; base plate connection at
spine; and glass curtain wall at spine.
/ Final design of: cafe at employee
entry; building two at slope curtain
wall; curtain wall/window wall juncture;
window wall/curtain wall juncture; and
cafe entry at building three.

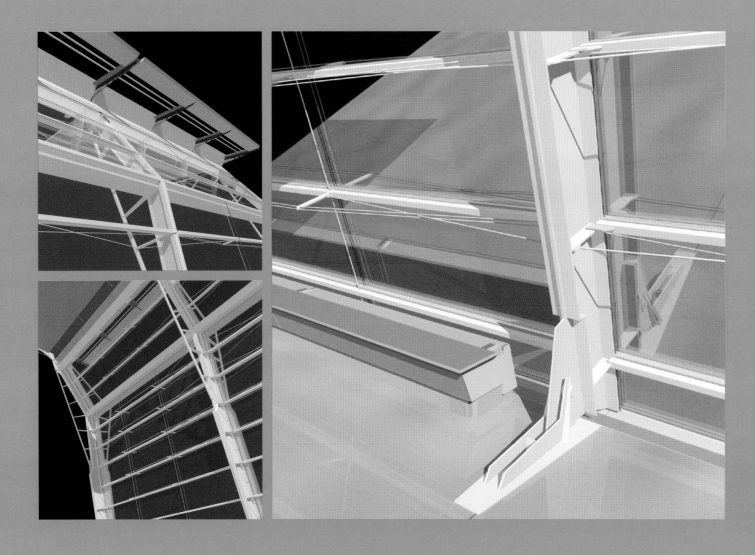

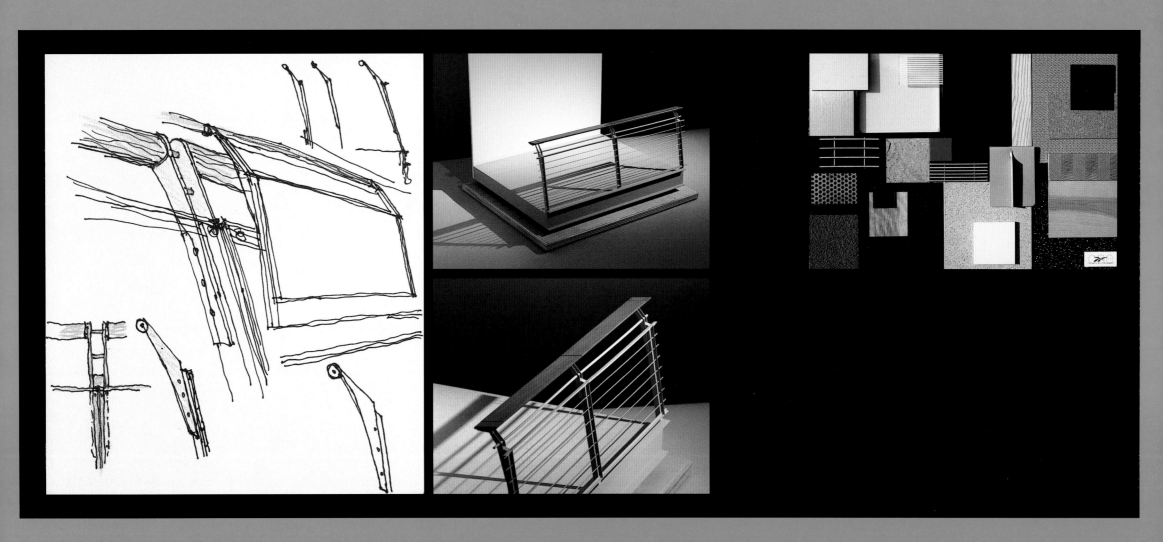

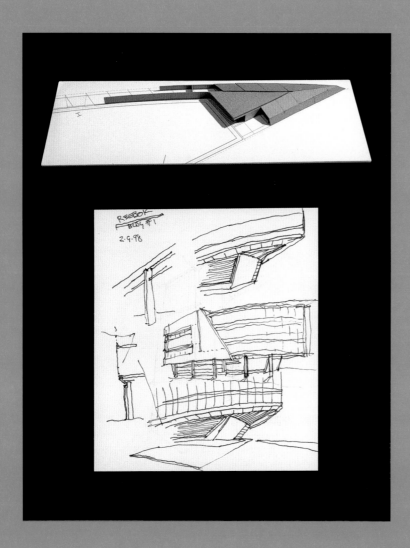

below / opposite page Design development entrance portico
and canopy model views. / Digital
images of spine and spine structure
development.

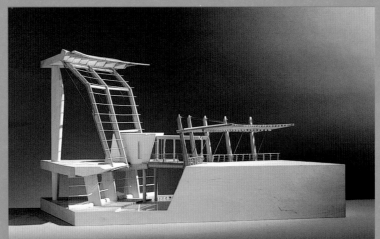

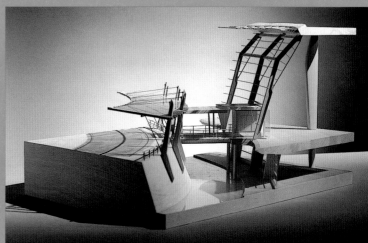

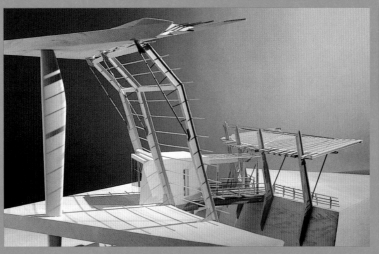

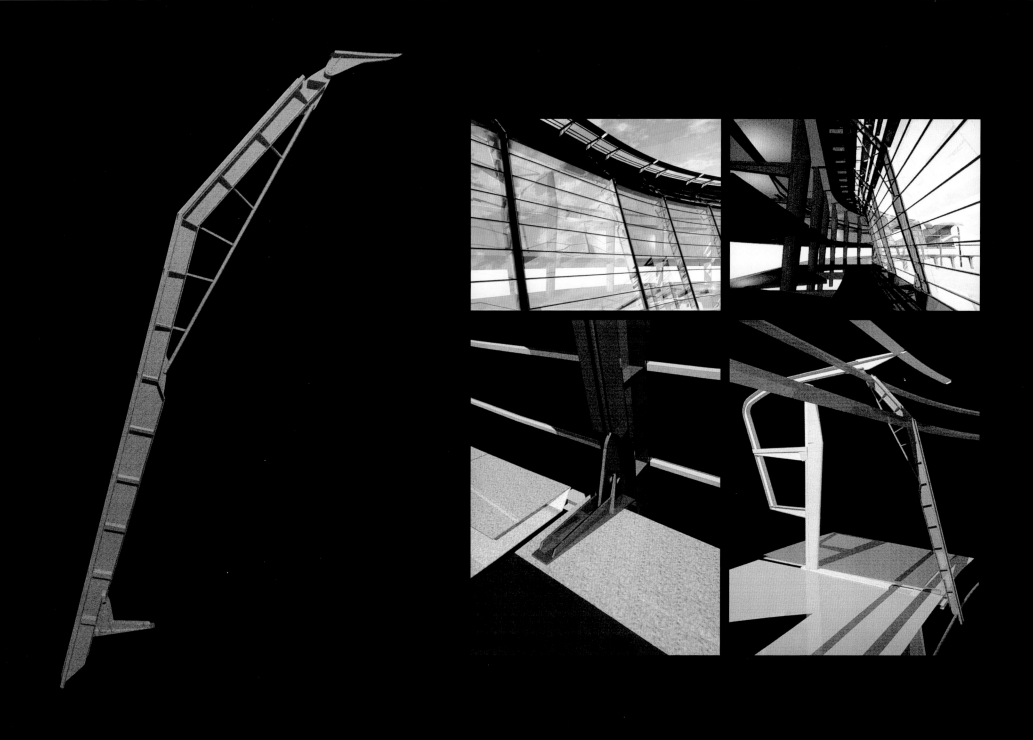

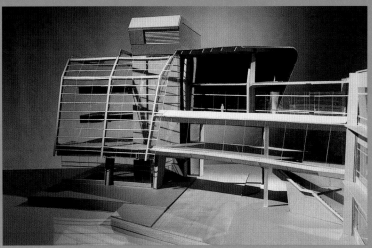

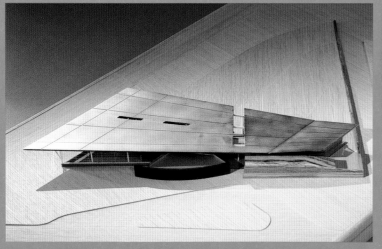

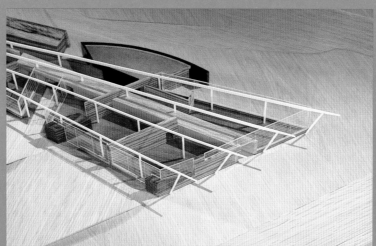

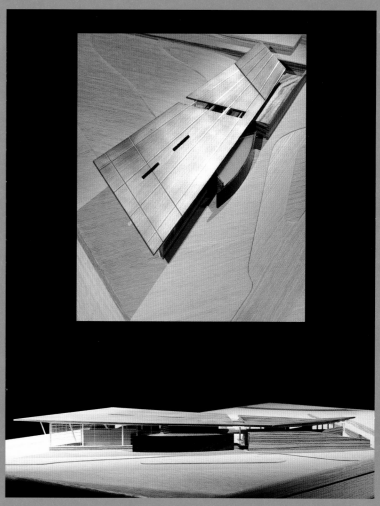

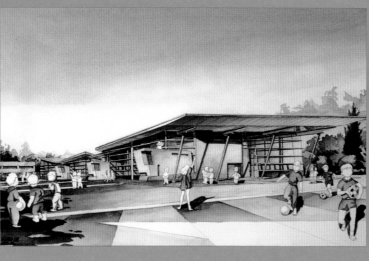

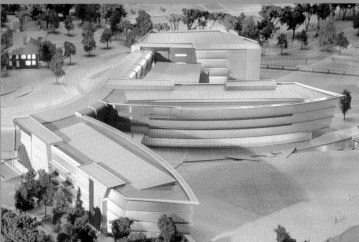

below / opposite page Sequential schematic design and
design development physical models
built by NBBJ's team. / Final
schematic exterior illustration by
William Hook.

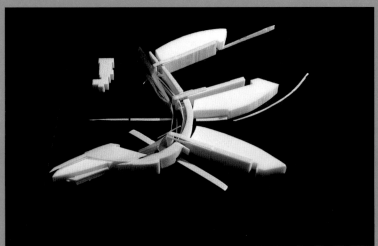

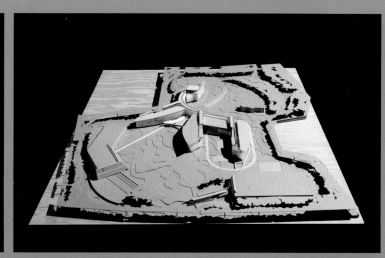

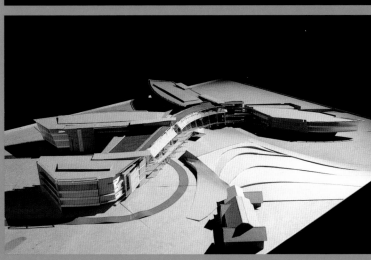

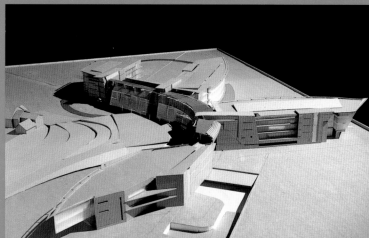

below (clockwise from top left) / opposite page   Concept site plan with final schematic
landscape vision, and physical and digital
models of concurrent spine developments.
/ Spine alternative concepts.

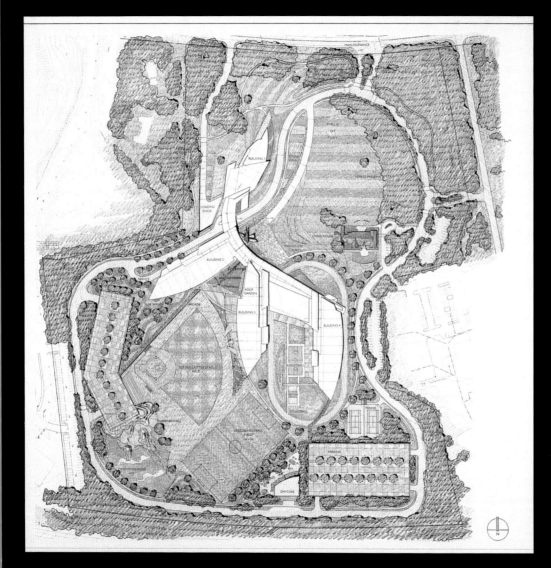

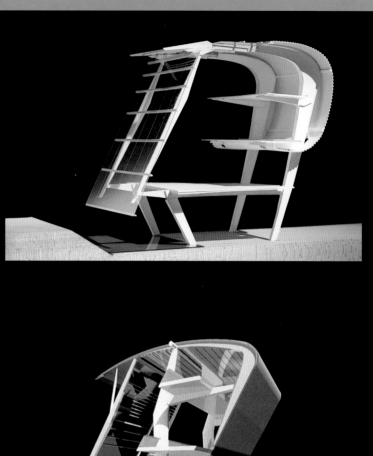

Following the rapid turnaround of the competition, the task of completing the project continued as a highly focused eight-month design sprint. "We immediately assigned twenty additional architects to the project," says Rob Swartz, NBBJ principal. "We established ownership of key areas and continued non-stop. We were on a mission." ■ What made the intensity of the process feasible was the cohesive energy and commitment of the design team. Everyone brought ideas and expertise to the table, allowing the design team to collaborate and form a deep bond. This passion for and sense of connection to the project became integral to the design, as the team members shared in the vision even while they were concurrently involved in separate functions. ■ At the same time, the use of advanced design technology provided for a new level of creativity and production acumen. Sophisticated three-dimensional computer software enabled mastery of the building's complex geometries. Normally, twice the time allotted would have been required to complete the design process. ■ "During the design of the headquarters, our goal was to create a living model," says Jonathan Ward, NBBJ senior project designer. "This gave us the chance to view, refine and test our ideas over and over again. The model was literally alive and growing at all times." ■ Unlike traditional two-dimensional renderings, NBBJ's 3-D schematic designs allowed Reebok executives to experience the concept for the headquarters true to form. NBBJ's animation capabilities provided for a virtual journey inside the model to visualize spaces from multiple perspectives. Aside from the

clear benefits to Reebok, the 3-D strategy afforded the ability to test and verify the complex spatial and material qualities of the overall design. This made it possible for NBBJ to control costs and effectively manage construction needs. ■ The strict eight-month time limitation for delivery of the design necessitated a creative process where designing never stopped, from initiation of the concept to completion of the construction documents. The architects maintained a high level of commitment, and were met in equal measure by their counterparts at Reebok who encouraged open communication. Foremost, Reebok wanted its employees to enjoy natural light. The building plan acknowledges this goal with high ceilings, open plan offices, and relatively narrow office wings. ■ Additionally, Reebok sought in-house opportunities to test products that are under development. Along with the regulation-size basketball court that is the centerpiece of the 30,000-square-foot fitness center, the designers included a small basketball floor with built-in force plates that measure the pressure exerted by players as they move across the court. ■ The central feature of the design vision, however, is the sinuous four-story, glass curtain wall horizontally spanning 350 feet—suggesting an Olympic stadium in form and serving as a circulation spine that ties the entire structure together. Faceted and supported by tension cables, the transparency of the spine blurs the distinction between inside and outside, bringing employees in touch with activities on the seven outdoor playing fields, the running track, and the indoor basketball court. The spine achieves a connection

between the actual creation of athletic products and their purpose in the larger world. To this end, the spine provides both an aesthetic and practical relevance to the overall project. ■ "The spine is anthropomorphic. Sectionally, it mirrors a very specific fraction of time when a runner's body is arched in the starting blocks. The spine's tensioned cable system and curved glass refer to tendons and muscles at the instant that the starting gun has gone off. The body is not quite in motion, yet it isn't stationary. It's a moment of explosion. This is the energy we want the structure to exude," says Jonathan Ward. ■ Beyond the structure's symbolic renderings, the design also achieves a powerful energy in practical terms. The open feel and undulating shape of the curtain wall encourages Reebok employees to interact. Balancing the significant amount of steel and glass within the spine, NBBJ designers utilized warm natural wood finishes such as maple flooring and cherry handrails on the balconies and stairs. ■ NBBJ's goal for the Reebok complex was to create a center where people can incorporate the company's high standards for creativity, collaboration, and explosive energy into their lifestyles. Though highly conceptual, this vision was achieved through practical methodology and smart technology. On-site amenities such as a fitness center, cafeteria, bank, company store and childcare facility allow Reebok employees to coalesce their work-a-day and personal lives. This environment has become the creative domain that inspires the evolution of Reebok's products, revitalizing the company's business culture and brand identity.

process

chapter three

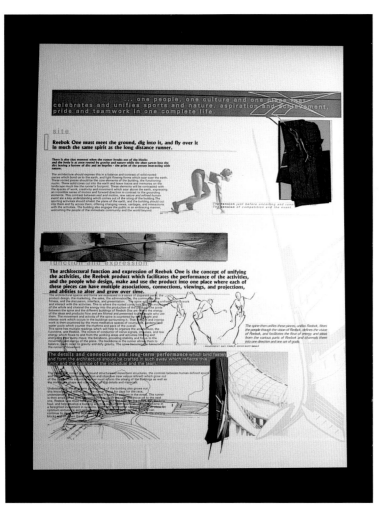

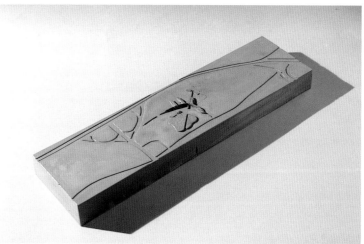

one

The Reebok World Headquarters

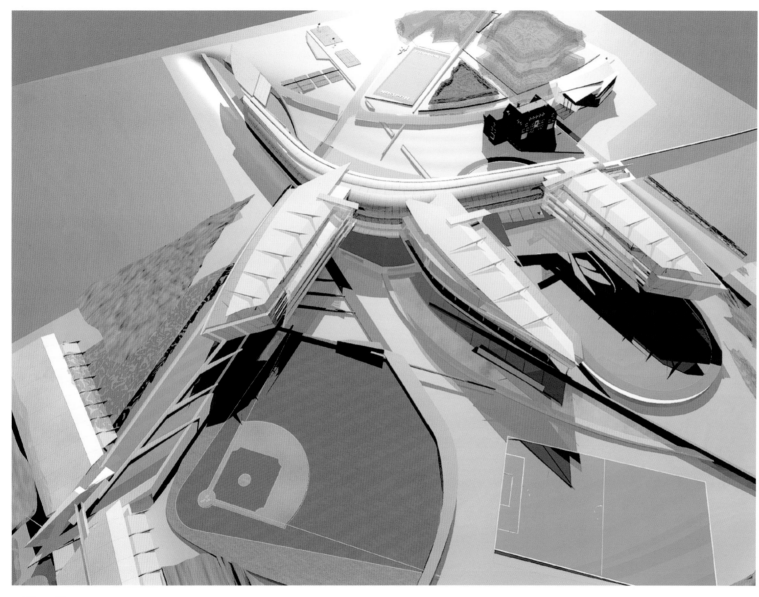

forty eight competition

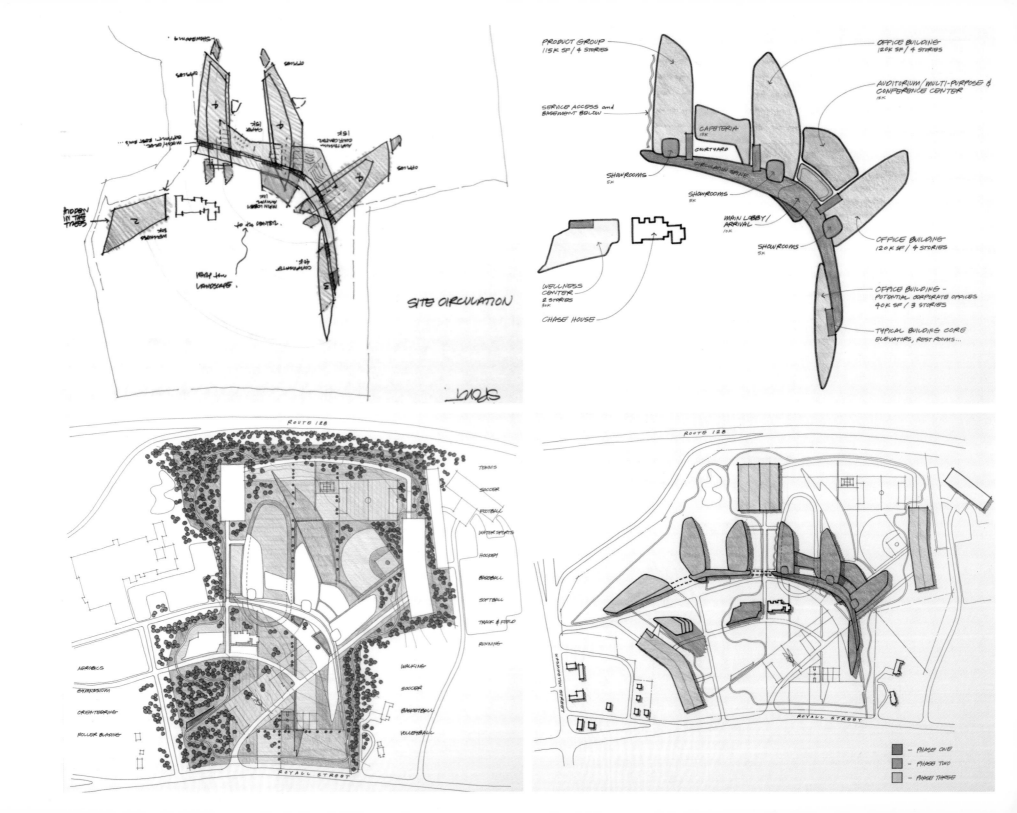

SITE CIRCULATION

PRODUCT GROUP
115K SF / 4 STORIES

OFFICE BUILDING
120K SF / 4 STORIES

SERVICE ACCESS and
BASEMENT BELOW

AUDITORIUM / MULTI-PURPOSE &
CONFERENCE CENTER
15K

CAFETERIA
15K

COURTYARD

CIRCULATION SPINE

SHOWROOMS
5K

SHOWROOMS
5K

MAIN LOBBY /
ARRIVAL
10K

OFFICE BUILDING
120K SF / 4 STORIES

SHOWROOMS
5K

WELLNESS
CENTER
2 STORIES
30K

CHASE HOUSE

OFFICE BUILDING -
POTENTIAL CORPORATE OFFICES
40K SF / 3 STORIES

TYPICAL BUILDING CORE
ELEVATORS, REST ROOMS...

ROUTE 128

TENNIS
SOCCER
FOOTBALL
WATER SPORTS
HOCKEY
BASEBALL
SOFTBALL
TRACK & FIELD
RUNNING

WALKING
SOCCER
BASKETBALL
VOLLEYBALL

AEROBICS
GYMNASIUM
ORIENTEERING
ROLLER BLADING

ROYALL STREET

ROUTE 128

WASHINGTON STREET

ROYALL STREET

■ - PHASE ONE
■ - PHASE TWO
□ - PHASE THREE

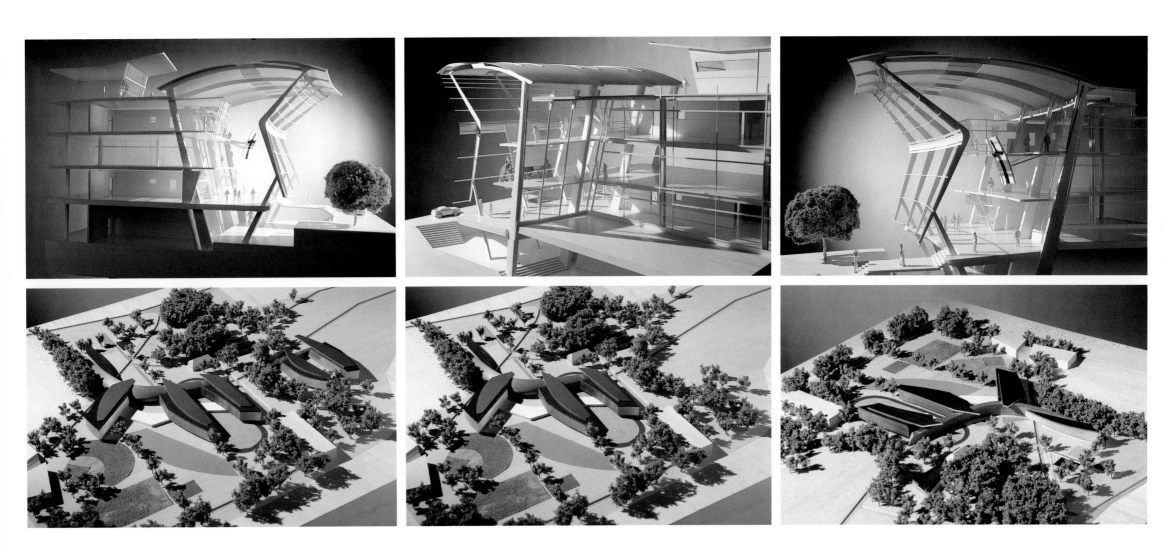

below (clockwise from top left) Three spine concept model views; northeast and southwest model views of initial phase; and southwest model view showing future expansion scenario. / Sequential site plan conceptual development including site circulation, organization diagram, landscape concept, and future growth diagram.

below (reverse clockwise from top right) / Reebok DMX technology inspiration and
opposite page   three conceptual idea models. / Digital
model, spine exterior and entrance view.

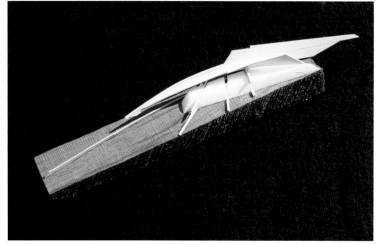

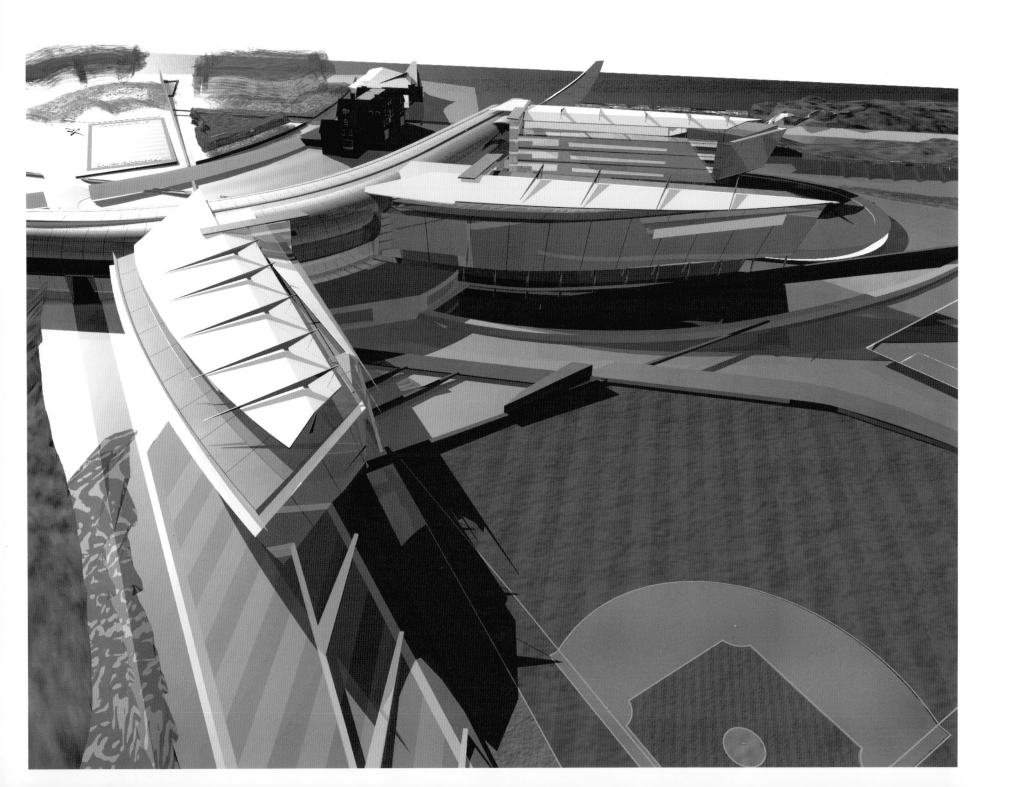

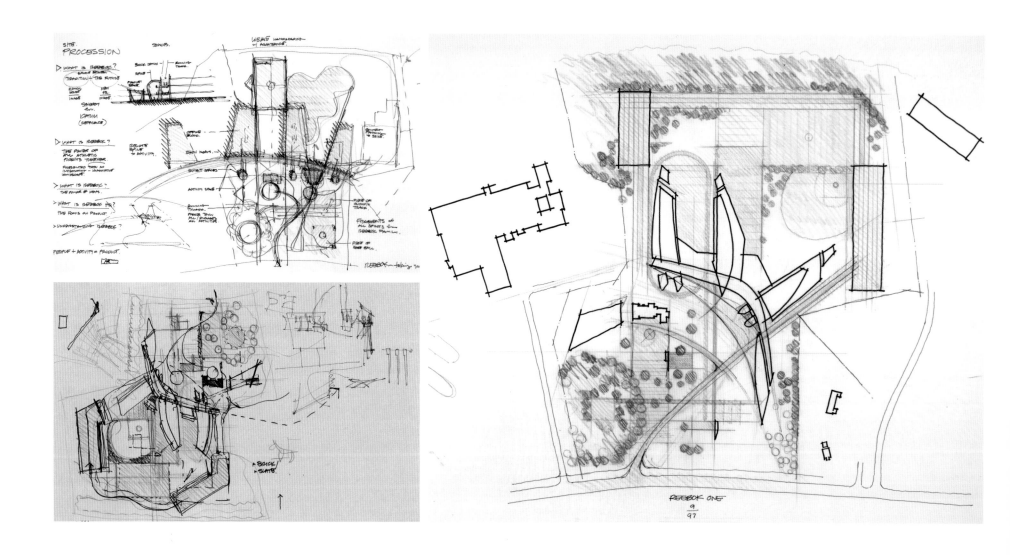

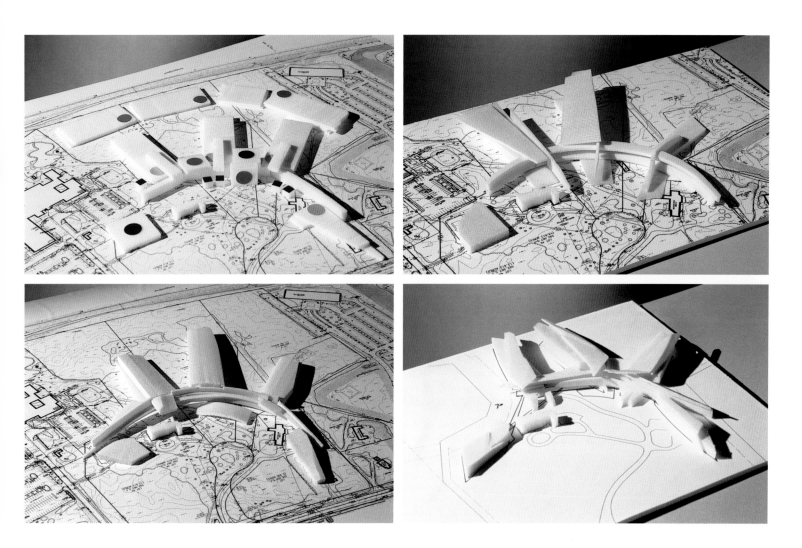

ACTIVITY   PRODUCT   PEOPLE

REEBOK
ONE

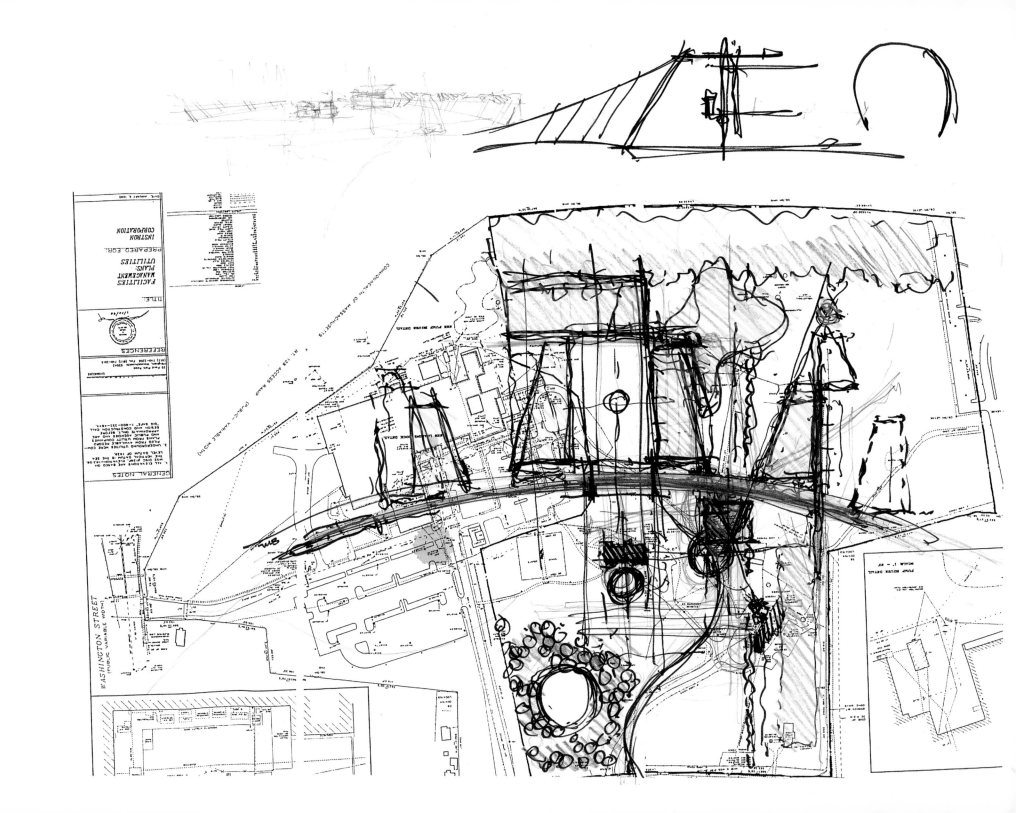

below / opposite page Preliminary sketches of idea-concepts
and notions of motion, and four early
site development strategies. / Early
site development alternative.

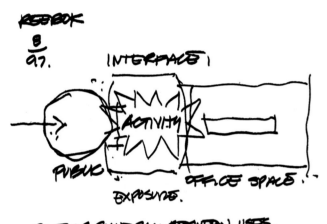

RSEBOK
8/97.

INTERFACE

ACTIVITY

PUBLIC

OFFICE SPACE

EXPOSURE.

DEVELOP SYNERGY BETWEEN USES.

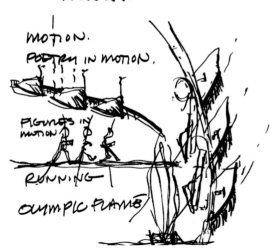

MOTION.

POETRY IN MOTION.

FIGURES IN MOTION

RUNNING

OLYMPIC FLAME

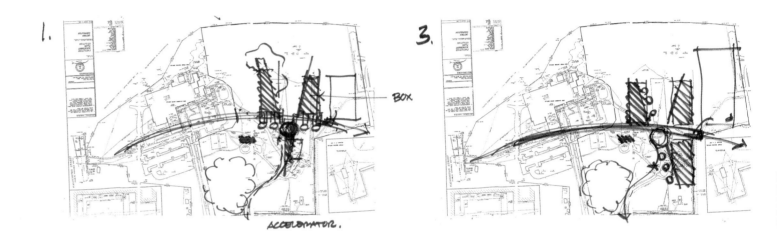

1.

BOX

ACCELERATOR.

2.

3.

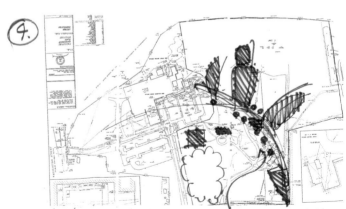

4.

THEMES: SPORTS
"OLYMPICS"
ENTERTAINMENT...

An invited competition to design the new headquarters challenged NBBJ to shape Reebok's vision of the future. Beginning with an intensive brainstorming session, NBBJ devised the concept of One. This became the driving, unifying concept that fueled the competition and ultimately determined the nature of Reebok's inspirational new workplace. ■ "What is the character of a place that will design exceptional sports products?" asked Scott Wyatt, NBBJ CEO. "It's an informal environment that stitches together the people and activities that Reebok creates products for." ■ Based on its collaborative and team-oriented culture, NBBJ had organized a multidisciplinary charrette within hours of meeting Reebok executives. The designers brought together specialists in architecture, landscape design, physical and digital modeling, and real estate development. ■ Concepts from each perspective were added simultaneously, as a rapid eight-day deadline did not allow for a traditional linear process. "Our ability to realize a compelling design vision within this timeframe was made possible through genuine interactive collaboration," says Steve McConnell, NBBJ Design Principal. "It was all about the best ideas." ■ The design team immediately felt a commonality with the notion that a new headquarters could refocus Reebok's sports and fitness culture. They recognized that the roots of productivity were the same for Reebok as for themselves, deeply embedded in the creative process. This meant identifying and making tangible the company's sources of inspiration that, for any design-based profession, benefit from a diversity of ideas and opportunities for cross-referencing.

■ After roughly a week of intensive development, NBBJ had the winning concept in place. Rather than bring multiple schemes to the table, the architects decided to present a single, profound design through which Reebok could revitalize itself. One served as the metaphor to embody Reebok's dynamic values and creativity. One would reflect the whole as the amalgamation of the body, mind and heart of the company. ■ Every detail was aimed at unifying Reebok's workforce and providing a platform for creativity. The design model focused on the fusion of Reebok's products with the activities they promote. To that effect, playing fields, an indoor basketball court, a running track that loops through the building, and a fitness center were incorporated directly into the building and site. ■ Using sophisticated computer software, the team manipulated complex curves to create the building's dynamic forms while individual elements were isolated for in-depth study and refinement. A transparent structural glass spine became the concept's central feature, a kind of main street linking four office wings and setting the stage for corporate esprit. McConnell explains, "We wanted the spine to have a vital activity and flow so that when you are in it you know this is Reebok!" ■ In claiming a single design concept, NBBJ mirrored Reebok's bold commitment to create a transformational headquarters. Like Reebok, NBBJ's shot at success had no safety net. Additionally, the competition had challenged the architects to deal with an international corporate identity, building on its existing message while simultaneously striving to make it new. Unlike starting with a clean slate,

this meant uncovering the means to acknowledge and reinvigorate a public brand. ■ "Our design represents the same integrity inherent in the ideals of Reebok," says Rick Buckley, NBBJ Design Partner. "What we brought to the table was a concept that allowed Reebok to reach its potential and see itself in its purest form." ■ The origins of inspiration often begin with one's environment. Reebok sought a structure that would embody the very nature of its goals: efficiency, creativity, boldness, energy, power, beauty. The new Reebok headquarters realizes these aspirations.

competition

chapter two

Current NBBJ work in progress builds on the "high-performance" architecture that defines the Reebok world headquarters. ST Asia Tower, Taipei, China; The Residences at Liberty, Jersey City, New Jersey, USA; Kwun Tong mixed-use development, Hong Kong, China; Dogus Maslak, Istanbul, Turkey; Kuwait Foundation for the Advancement of Sciences, Kuwait City, Kuwait; Seoul Dome, Seoul, South Korea. / Telenor Headquarters, Oslo, Norway.

below / opposite page Reebok's United Kingdom-based ancestor was founded for one of the best reasons possible: athletes wanted to run faster. / Joseph William Foster of Bolton, England, a keen runner and member of the Bolton Primrose Harriers, wanted a pair of spiked running shoes. With money in short supply, he built his own in 1895. It was the first pair of "Foster" running shoes. In 1958 Joseph's grandsons, renamed their grandfather's company "Reebok" after the South African gazelle.

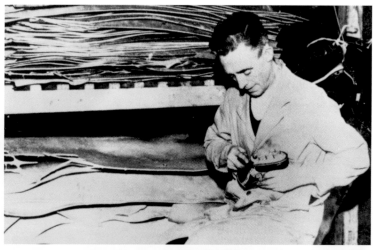

The most creative and innovative companies recognize the strategic importance of their workplace environments. The right setting attracts and retains the best talent. An inspiring workplace promotes drive and enthusiasm. At the start of the 21st century, Reebok seized an opportunity to create a new world headquarters that would refocus and re-energize its workforce and identity. ■ Rarely is an enterprising endeavor of this scope undertaken during a cyclic downturn. In the mid-1990s, Reebok, originators of the athletic products made famous by the emergence of aerobics into mainstream culture, had leveled off both creatively and financially. The effects of this trend were felt externally and internally as the company's market share declined. In order to reawaken its potential, Reebok sought the means once more to claim the company's entrepreneurial spirit of adventure. ■ Despite the significant risk involved, Paul Fireman, President and CEO of Reebok, realized the chance to revitalize an entire company and surge the athletic market with innovation. What emerged from his vision was the understanding that in order to grow and evolve, the company would have to make a bold statement. Fireman determined, "I don't want an office building. I want a place that is the spirit of innovation." ■ For Reebok, however, building a new world headquarters was not simply an artistic venture resting on conceptual goals; real, quantifiable figures were required. Cost efficiency, work productivity, minimizing employee attrition, and establishing a recruiting tool were primary objectives. To that effect, the design could not be

boilerplate. Every detail had to reflect and reinforce the company's business needs and dynamic creative values. ■ As part of an intense design competition, Reebok challenged NBBJ to create an architectural vision that reflects the essence of the company. To NBBJ this meant an environment where the energy and excitement of sports and fitness are ever present. The architects produced a concept that would transform the way Reebok employees work and think about work. ■ NBBJ devised a place that connects all aspects of Reebok's business: the people, the products and the athleticism. Certain components were considered essential to the company's health-conscious culture, such as physical activity, access to nature, daylight, fresh air, and on-site childcare. Taking these lifestyle elements into account, the space embodies Reebok's spirit of innovation and collaboration, and promotes success by fostering the well-being of everyone involved. ■ On a 44-acre rural site, the 520,000-square-foot structure rises four stories in an arena-like setting, surrounded by seven outdoor athletic fields and activity areas of various types. By weaving sports and fitness facilities around and through the headquarters, the design connects employees to the sights, sounds and energy that inspire their work. ■ It is a new type of workplace that integrates all aspects of the business, bringing together the employees and their culture of athleticism with Reebok's products and their intended uses. NBBJ interpreted the concept of corporate campus as implying an interconnected complex. With a fitness center at its heart, it is a single structure that radiates

energy and open communication. . ■ Throughout the day, the interior and exterior athletic facilities thrive with the activity of employees whose first-hand knowledge of sports helps to hone innovative solutions for the equipment they design. This project is a testament to the fact that buildings can help to define and coalesce a company's understanding of itself. The image of architecture becomes synonymous with the image of the company. Reebok's new world headquarters integrates people's sports and fitness lifestyles with the company's identity, and inspires employees to push themselves with the same energy that is embodied in the architecture.

beginnings

on elevators, with a shop, cafe, restaurant, basketball court, visitors' desk and, at one end, the conference center. Extra unprogrammed space is used for receptions and exhibitions. Physically the space is highly porous, with balconies and cutouts in the floors allowing views down to the lowest levels. The concourse, organized with relaxed rather than rigid geometries, is not monolithic and directive. ■ It has often been said that the free and creative exchange of ideas in many institutions occurs during chance encounters between people passing on corridors and in stairwells. Designing the building to proliferate such serendipitous meetings, the architects act as social engineers rigging corridors so that someone from marketing, say, on his way to Starbucks in the basement, bumps into someone from design, on her way to the Judo class. She in turn runs into someone from research on his way to the ATM in back of the cafeteria, where they both meet others dropping off their lunch trays. Elements like the company store act as magnets. The chance encounters not only spark ideas but also foster a sense of community. ■ The architects are basically urbanizing the suburban office building with systems of circulation and an enriched program of activity. The interior life may be unique by current office park standards, but it takes up the tradition of the multi-functional Downtown Athletic Club that Rem Koolhaas described in "Delirious New York," which effectively operated as a small high-rise town: its mixed activities range from hotel to gym to oyster bar. Architecturally, NBBJ's town-in-a-building allows more interaction than the Downtown Athletic Club because the building is more open and less

stratified, and the architects purposely cultivate a sense of energy through sports. "What is Reebok?" asks McConnell. "It's the energy created by sports and fitness activities throughout the headquarters, like the runners flashing by through the glass tunnel a level below you." ■ Though complex and rich, the organizational concept did not mean the architects could simply extrude the building up from the diagram. The concourse might hyphenate the pods, but the diagram was not yet a building. Reebok did not yet have its landmark structure. ■ The designers looked for architectural expression in metaphor. At a macro scale, the architects conceived the façade as a curved segment of a stadium amphitheater, focused on the entry court. "The idea was that when you arrived at Reebok you would feel the exhilaration of gazing up at a stadium bowl from the 50 yard line," says McConnell. Other formal gestures evolved from the concept of the partial amphitheater, including the lead-coated copper shoulder on the back façade. "Once you start curving the spine and extending its arc, you set up a complexity that ripples throughout the building," says Swartz. "And the curves raise questions: how do they end? how do the office pods interact with the spine? The curves increased the complexity throughout, at all levels of architectural issues—materials, geometries, finishes." ■ At the micro scale, the architects looked to the human body. But the body in question was not Leonardo's proportional drawing of the man in the circle inscribed in the square, or Corbusier's Modulor Man. It was the runner, muscles tensed, feet in the block, at the moment the gun has gone off. Notions of physical tension

and stretching worked their way into the design of the curtain wall along the concourse, the most technically advanced part of the building. ■ A four-story curved glass façade angled to the sky requires a lot of steel, but conventional steel columns could well have smothered the openness, so the designers and their curtain wall structural engineer ASI "Advanced Structures Incorporated" devised a horizontal truss system that suspended the glazing. The cross-cable truss extends from one end of the concourse to the other and works as a continuous tension structure. To lighten its appearance, the architects borrowed structural concepts from the body, and studied how the tendons work with bones, diverting stresses. The structuration eliminated visually obstructive steel columns, so that the interior space, with a sloped front wall, now belongs to the sky: when you stand inside the corridor, you see through the glass with little interference from the steel. The structural concept helps achieve the architectural goal of dematerializing the border between outside and inside. On the inboard side of the concourse, the architects shaped fiberglass sheathed columns like bones, expressing the forces they carry, so the structure along the concourse, rather than looking like a colonnade, acquired an anatomy that echoed the tensed body of the runner at the block. ■ Meanwhile, the architects opened the space above the concourse floor to the roof, and at times removed pieces of the floor, for overlooks onto the red track passing beneath the belly of the concourse. The sectional richness contributes to the sense of community not only because of eye contact, but because of the acoustics. The squeak of Reebok shoes on the basketball court can be

heard down the corridor, an aleatoric Cagian noise giving the interior the scale of friendly, recognizable sounds associated with school and community gyms. ■ The architects may celebrate this public space, but they do not ignore the office pods. To open up the wings and channel pedestrian energy toward the concourse, the architects situate the elevators and firestairs in a knuckle where the wings join the concourse: people, air, data, electricity all move through this connection. The architects express the core's presence by detailing the plans as though the wing were grabbing, or stapling, the concourse. An elaborate basement, much like the one at Disney World or in any major luxury hotel, is hidden behind the scenes and supports the upper floors. At the perimeter of each wing, a long arc runs the length of each pod on one side, accelerating the form and space of the open office plan. The arc ends in a glass wall tilted toward the playing fields, like a press box at a stadium. The building is spectator to the sports it encourages. ■ From the outside, the curves of the façades play off the straight walls and off each other, as in a winding country road that gives rotational views of the landscape. Because of the revolving curves, and the highly differentiated façade, driving, running, or walking around the building reveals a building with a constantly changing relationship between its own parts, the playing field, and the landscape. The parallactic shifts continue inside for the same reasons but at a different scale. "When you're moving, you can see three or five parts at the same time, and you constantly feel the building is always changing as you move around," says Park. The basic visual metaphor of the building,

movement, itself encourages locomotion outside and inside as the building takes on shifting perspectival views. ■ Conceptually rich, metaphorically strong, formally tensed, the building also expresses the larger ideas and ideals at a smaller scale, in the materials and the details. The slanted glass façade may make people look up to the sky, but the architects ground the building in a sensuous material world, with maple floors and ceilings, cherry handrails, concrete treads, and variously patterned carpets. The concourse is richly dressed, with woods and textiles that give warmth to the steel-and-glass environment. The materiality, however, is not gratuitously decorative. The carpets are cut and inlaid to extend the larger curved and angular geometries underlying the building, and their arcs and slashed patterns bring the dynamic lines that run through the building into the concourse. The decoration leads the eye to understand the large and small forces tying together the interior and exterior. Like the landscape, the floors are conceived as interactive fields; the notion of dynamic athleticism informs the graphics of the plan and interior promenade. ■ Complexity, recently, has been misunderstood as a new kind of formalism—often handsome and even intriguing, like a puzzle, but self-referential. NBBJ's complexity at Reebok, however, represents a value system. Like the human personality, corporate life is a complex, layered construct, and the architectural layering of the building corresponds to the many strata of issues in Reebok's corporate life. ■ Since IBM championed architecture in the 1950s and 1960s with a deliberate program of architectural excellence, designers have

built many corporate icons. With its figural plan and figural façade, Reebok headquarters is indeed iconic: this is a building people can point to. But there is a wisdom embedded in the complexity. On one hand, the design represents a gesture of generosity to the employees, and on the other, a call to creativity. Bold and conspicuously enthusiastic, the building is, psychologically, a winner, and by its example, it raises the bar for creativity and aesthetic risk within the ranks. This is high-achievement, high-performance, can-do architecture that gives Reebok's corporate culture an environmental equivalent. ■ Furthermore, the architects have used Reebok's raison d'être, sports, and its corporate philosophy, the spirit of camaraderie generated by sports, as a driving metaphor for creating a sense of community. Working as a social catalyst, the building opens channels of communication that nourish the corporate operations and the collective psyche. In the wisest sense, the new headquarters is an enabler because the building encourages the performance of the company itself. This is a building people not only want to see but also work in. In the isolating, car-oriented world of the beltway, the design offers a new paradigm of a building that is both urban and suburban—an integrated cityscape and landscape that cultivates the activities that forge and bind a community.

Joseph Giovanninni,
New York, October 2001

The genie of architectural complexity slipped out of the Brancusi bottle in the early 1980s, defying the conventional wisdom that modernism, to be modernist, had to be pure and simple. The argument for complexity was at first proposed by young architects doing boutique projects, but a fresh generation of monumental buildings has recently captured the lens, the press, and the imagination of the traveling public. Architecture tourists are enthusiastically leaving their home entertainment centers to visit new buildings that qualify as international events. ■ Despite their open and gestural forms, most of these new structures are self-contained designs with a cool relationship to the surrounding landscape: though they may be geometrically liberated, they hardly reach beyond their walls to engage and cultivate their sites. Unique among the new monuments, however, is Reebok International's headquarters outside Boston. With four four-story wings angling off a main circulation concourse, the building stretches into the surrounding acreage, inviting the grounds and playing fields into an embrace that blurs the distinction between landscape and building. This is not an isolated object sitting on a groomed lawn, but a building that belongs to its site like an athlete doing stretching exercises. ■ Corporate America is well populated with architectural logos that lend their silhouettes to corporate image. In suburbs, these objects sit passively in office parks—boxes perched on manicured planes of grass next to squares of parking. But Reebok headquarters, in Canton, just two turns off Boston's high-tech Route 128, plays a participatory role in an activity landscape. A running track and a vehicular roadway

both cross the site under lifted sections of the building, and a baseball diamond and soccer field slide into spaces defined by the reaching arms. ■ Visitors and staff drive up to and under the building as they head to the garage at the rear of the property and then walk back past the playing fields to the back entry. Taxis turn off the same road and ramp up a mound to drop other visitors off at a heroic glass canopy at the front entrance. ■ Inside, the architects program the glassy three-story corridor that links the wings with a restaurant, cafe, store, reception desk, basketball court and gym. The concourse works like a Main Street in an American town, drawing out the residents and focusing the community in a space that Revolutionary Russian architects once called a "social condenser." Conferences and lectures take place in an auditorium at one end, where a two-level lobby doubles, above and below, as an exhibition space. The indoor and outdoor public spaces function all year round as stages for Reebok's numerous special events, from fireworks to reggae concerts. Strategizing organization and space, the architects choreograph urban spontaneity. Generic buildings in office parks often straightjacket occupants, bringing all parts of the operation to heel in a single geometric form— usually a rectangular prism or cube. NBBJ designed a complex building for the complex nature of Reebok. The architects articulated the moving parts of the corporation within a complex whole without repressing them within a simple, and simplistic, overriding geometry. Using discreet parts as their building blocks, the architects acknowledge the diversity of the company. The resulting design, then,

is not just a monofunctional 9-to-5 office box, like so many of the corporate neighbors that ring Boston on 128, but a small town with an interior urban life set among the playing fields in the surrounding landscape. Deploying functions strategically, they catalyze an interior townscape, casting the occupants as players and citizens in an active spatial field. Occupants are not simply commuters tethered to their cars but a community, people enjoying multiple roles—working, exercising, conferencing, dining, socializing, gallery going, shopping, convenience banking. With its dynamized forms and a glass façade structured on tensed cables, the design itself is aesthetically proactive, an object lesson for designers who occupy the building. The design is both motivational and inspirational. ■ The story of the commission started with the end of the lease in office buildings that offered only a bland presence and little sense of place and corporate identity. The previous buildings were static designs, and as a scattered group, they failed to tie the company together. After a recent slide in Reebok's share in an intensely competitive market, its management, under the direction of CEO Paul Fireman and corporate real estate head Douglas Noonan, realized that a landmark building, among other measures, could help recharge the company and its culture. After a false start with another architectural firm, Reebok staged an invited competition, asking for a bold vision rather than a traditional architectural approach and site strategy. "They were looking for new headquarters to unify them in a way they hadn't been," says Scott Wyatt, Managing Partner of NBBJ. "The company was re-energizing itself."

■ "When we analyzed the company, we found that innovation and technology were key elements to Reebok's operation," says Robert Swartz, an NBBJ principal with a background in commercial real estate. "Research based in technology became the early building blocks for the design charrettes. How do you incorporate athleticism, innovation and technology into a building?" ■ Reebok, as a voice in sports culture, espouses athletic community, with an emphasis on teamwork rather than hero worship. "A big part of the task was to create a place where creative products could happen through collaboration between product designers," says Wyatt. Reebok's commitment to design excellence meant conceiving a building that optimized the process of collaborative design. In this spirit, the architects themselves banded together in a team that allowed them to address a complex of concerns with specific expertise, ranging from corporate psychologist to form-giver. Besides Wyatt and Swartz, the core of the NBBJ team included: design principal in charge of the project, Steven McConnell; senior project designer Jonathan Ward; project designers Jin Ah Park and Andy Bromberg; technical designer Nick Charles; interior designers Chris Larson and Alan Young; construction administration lead Ruben Gonzalez; and Richard Buckley, partner-in-charge of design (competition). ■ Uniquely sited between Route 128 and Great Blue Hill, the highest point in the area, the 42-acre property was large enough that the field games did not have to be tightly packed, but could be separate and distinct from each other. The architects chose, however, to densify and intensify the site: they wanted to provoke synergy by conceiving the field events and building as overlap-

ping, interactive precincts. From the beginning, then, the diagram of the building involved the diagram of the site—and in a sectional, three-dimensional way. Lifting the main parts of the building above grade allowed the architects to bring the site under and through the building, establishing continuities at and above ground level. A roadway from the entry ramps up to an entry podium, which is sided with huge granite foundation blocks retrieved from Boston's Big Dig. Several fingers, or pods, housing the offices stretch into the site, defining outdoor spaces and positioning themselves as box seats for sports events. The architects yoke work and play in an easy juxtaposition that explains Reebok's reciprocal attitudes about the business of sport and the sport of business. ■ "I've always been interested in how movement can impact a building, and how the movement of the place and its topography describe and inscribe the building," says Ward, who had previously worked in a similar vocabulary of ideas with NBBJ architect Peter Pran on a Florida project. "This was the perfect building for those ideas, at different scales, starting with the tapestry of the sports fields—the track, the diamond, the soccer field. We allowed the movements of the site to impact the program of the building and its diagram." Using the topography of movement as a design concept resonated with Reebok's product: sports equipment implies movement. ■ Inside, the pods lead like tributaries, or side streets, to the concourse, which collects the building's sights and sounds (including the patter of basketballs on the indoor court). The architects programmed the three-story corridor with a monumental staircase serving all floors, reducing dependency

introduction

by joseph giovanninni

contents

First published in Australia in 2002 by
The Images Publishing Group Pty Ltd
ABN 89 059 734 431

6 Bastow Place, Mulgrave, Victoria, 3170, Australia
Telephone: +61 3 9561 5544 Facsimile: +61 3 9561 4860
e-mail: books@images.com.au
website: www.imagespublishinggroup.com

The Images Publishing Group Reference Number: 491

National Library of Australia
Cataloguing-in-Publication data

Reebok World Headquarters NBBJ

ISBN: 1 87690 758 4

1. Reebok World Headquarters (Canton. Mass.). 2. NBBJ (Firm). 3.
Reebok International – Buildings. 4. Architecture – Massachusetts –
Canton – Design and plans.
1. Riera Ojeda, Oscar

720.9744

Printed in China by Palace Press

Designed by Oscar Riera Ojeda and Lucas H. Guerra
Layout: Oscar Riera Ojeda

reebok world headquarters nbbj

edited by oscar riera ojeda | introduction by joseph giovanninni

images
Publishing

reebok world headquarters **nbbj**